The OUTCOME Primers Series 2.0

The SUSTAINABILITY Primer

Other Books in This Series

THE SUSTAINABILITY PRIMER
SUSTAINING LEARNING OUTCOMES AND ASSESSMENT

Kathy Telban
President, Chief Outcome Strategist and Coach, iSOLVit LLC
Past Board Member, White Water Institute for Leadership Training
Former Director of Curriculum Development and Learning Outcome Assessment, Cuyahoga Community College

Ruth Stiehl
Founder, The Learning Organization
Professor Emeritus, Instructional Systems
Oregon State University

The Learning Organization

The SUSTAINABILITY Primer:
Sustaining Learning Outcomes and Assessment

Kathy Telban and Ruth Stiehl

First Edition Copyright © 2017
The Learning Organization
Corvallis, Oregon
Library of Congress Cataloging Number: 2016911675
ISBN: 978-1534887916

Executive Editor: Don Prickel
Assistant Editor: Lori Sours
Editor/Production: Robin McBride
Graphics and Illustrations: Katy Krupp

Printed in United States of America

CreateSpace Independent Publishing Platform, North Charleston, SC

For further information, visit our website at *www.outcomeprimers.com*
or email us at *strategists@outcomeprimers.com*.

To our families

—KT, RS

Table of Contents

PART THREE: Creating *and Sustaining an Outcomes and Assessment System through Effective Leadership*

Changing a whole system requires sustained leadership.

PART FOUR: *Creating and Sustaining an Outcomes and Assessment System through Instructor Involvement*

There is nothing more foundational to outcomes thinking than to carry a mental image of paddlers on a white-water journey through unfamiliar rapids with a guide at the back.

PART FIVE: *Creating and Sustaining an Outcomes and Assessment System through Professional Development*

The best part of learning is sharing what you know.

—Vaughn K. Lauer

PART SIX: *Creating and Sustaining an Outcomes and Assessment System through System Integration*

A complex system that works is invariably found to have evolved from a simple system that worked.

—John Gall

The Purpose of This Book Stated as a Learning Outcome

Working through this book should help build your capacity to:

Create and sustain an outcomes and assessment system through effective leadership, instructor involvement, professional development, and system integration.

The OUTCOME Primers Series 2.0

The OUTCOME Primer: *Envisioning Learning Outcomes*

What do learners need to be able to do in real-life roles that we are responsible for in programs, courses, and workshops?

The ASSESSMENT Primer: *Assessing and Tracking Evidence of Learning Outcomes*

What can learners do to show evidence of the intended outcomes and how will the evidence be documented, tracked, and used?

The CONTENT Primer: *Aligning Essential Content with Learning Outcomes*

What concepts, skills, and issues are essential for learners to achieve the intended outcomes?

The MAPPING Primer: *Mapping the Way to Learning Outcomes*

How do we assure that the learner's journey aligns with the intended outcomes?

The GUIDING Primer: *Guiding Toward Learning Outcomes*

What do effective *guides* do that is so different from our traditional notion of *teaching*?

The SUSTAINABILITY Primer: *Sustaining Learning Outcomes and Assessment*

How do we create a system of learning outcomes and assessment so the work is sustained?

Once a Fad—Now a Fact!

When we published the very first OUTCOMES Primer in the year 2000, academic and workplace training programs were deemed a success based on seat time, bodies in the seats, and the number of topics covered; the transfer of learning to real-life roles was little more than an afterthought.

It has taken the past fifteen years for professional organizations and accreditation agencies to move the adult education industry into adopting an outcome-based framework for curricular planning. Once a fad, now a fact, implementing curricula that are driven by clear and robust learning outcomes is a major challenge for all education programs in universities, community, and technical colleges, as well as the workplace.

It is one thing for an organization to *own* the idea of learning outcomes, and quite another for it to create a sustainable system that includes six key actions:

The six Essential Questions addressed in The OUTCOME Primers Series 2.0

- *What do learners need to be able to do in real-life roles that we are responsible for in programs, courses, and workshops?*

- *What can learners do to show evidence of the intended outcomes and how will the evidence be documented, tracked, and used?*

- *What concepts, skills, and issues are essential for the learners to achieve the intended outcomes?*

- *How do we assure that the learner's journey aligns with the intended outcomes?*

- *What do effective* guides *do that is so different from our traditional notion of "teaching"?*

- *How do we create a system of learning outcomes and assessment so the work is sustained?*

envisioning learning outcomes, aligning essential content with learning outcomes, assessing and tracking evidence of outcomes, mapping learning experiences, guiding learners toward the outcomes, and sustaining the process during other kinds of organizational change. Our newly released *OUTCOME Primers Series 2.0* is designed and structured to make every leader, instructor, and trainer proficient in these six areas of outcomes planning and assessment.

Distinguishing Our Work

If there were two primary things that distinguish our work with outcomes and assessment from all others, it would have to be the understanding of *outside-in* and *the learner's journey.*

In all six Primers, we have sought to apply systems thinking through the concept of *outside-in*—the simple notion that every learning experience is for a purpose outside the learning environment, meaning, in real life contexts. Planning for a learning experience begins *outside.*

The second thing that distinguishes our work in the Primers is the concept of *the learner's journey*. If there is any unifying visual organizer that can clarify outcome-based learning and assessment in academic and workplace organizations, it is a paddler on a rapidly flowing whitewater river. To us, there is nothing more foundational to outcomes thinking than to carry a mental image of learners on their journey in an ever-changing river of life experiences. In *The GUIDING Primer: Guiding Toward Learning Outcomes*, we reinforce this image by picturing a paddle raft of learners on a whitewater river with the guide at the back, where every rapid is an opportunity to assess learning.

When we envision a workshop, training, course, or program as a sequence of learning experiences that flow from the first class session, *the put-in*, to the last class session, *the take-out*, there seems to be greater clarity about what it means to teach, train, or GUIDE (our preferred word) toward significant outcomes. It is this image of the *learner's journey* and *outside-in* that we carry throughout all the six Primers in this series, and capture, in its simplest form, on the following pages. These two primary distinguishing characteristics of the Primers are illustrated in the overleaf on pages xviii and xix.

While our approach to understanding outcomes and assessment has not changed from our first primer in 2000, it is quite a departure for us to break outcomes planning into six distinct Primers (a *six-pac*). There are three specific reasons we have selected this small format for our new Series:

- Each Primer highlights one important element in outcome-based planning and can be used independently for intensive professional development.
- We can produce quantities of individual primers inexpensively, meaning organizations can afford to get them in the hands of every trainer and every instructor, not just the leaders.
- Each Primer or the entire series of six books (a *six-pac*) can be printed and shipped literally overnight.

As always, there are trade-offs in keeping the purchase price low and separating the tasks. We have chosen to forego our desire to use color, high-end paper, and fold-out pages. We also take a risk in separating each element of outcomes and assessment from the *whole*; all systems are greater than the individual parts taken separately. The answer is to invest in the *whole*.

It is our hope that these books will prove as useful as the original series we began more than 15 years ago.

—Ruth Stiehl
Corvallis, Oregon
2017

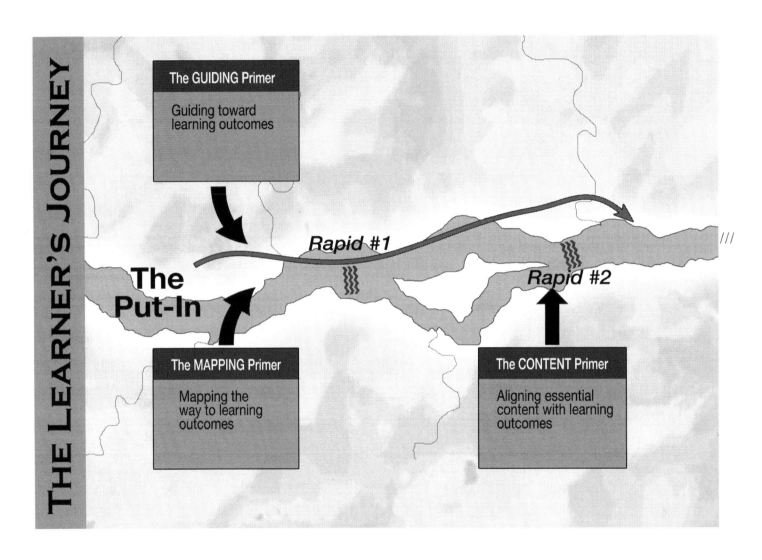

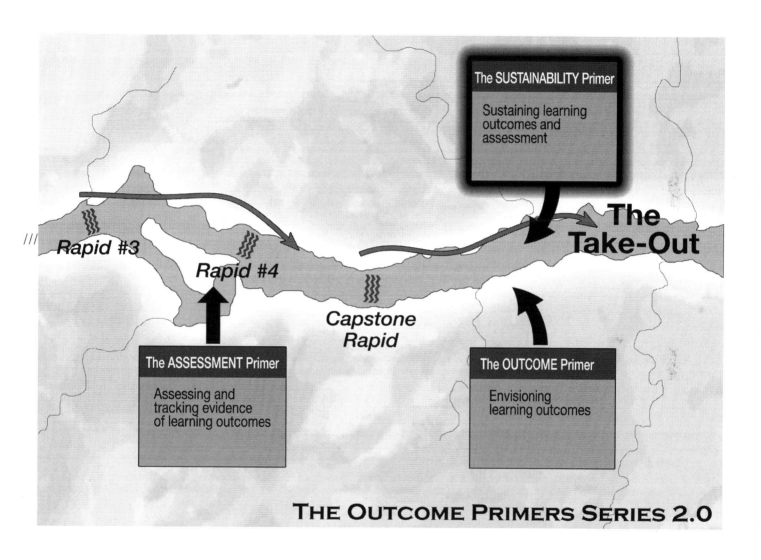

PART ONE:
Creating and Sustaining an Outcomes and Assessment Initiative

Sustainability arises from a flow of information through adjustment cycles.

Introduction: The Issue of Sustainability

Outcome-based education and assessment have been a focus of higher education for over two decades, yet it is still being cited in accreditation reports as a major concern that requires interim progress reporting.

For example: "University placed on notice by Higher Learning Commission" was the headline last year for one university that was found out of compliance with accreditation standards for outcomes and assessment efforts.

The letter, which was made public by a simple click to a linked pdf (thanks to the internet), clearly outlined several problems including the progress they needed to show in assessment of student learning outcomes. Needless to say, the online report generated a good deal of public concern about the status of the university. Unfortunately, this is not an uncommon case.

We may as well face it—much of the effort colleges and workplace certification programs have been doing with learning outcomes and assessment has been little more than a struggle to comply with standards imposed by certification or accreditation bodies. When an accreditation review is imminent, the work accelerates. When it's over, the work slows and sometimes even stops. In most colleges, it is not yet a natural, sustained practice at either the program or college-wide level. That's why, after fifteen years in this work of outcome-based curriculum design, we are still at it.

So, the question is: **How do we sustain the ground we have gained with learning outcomes and assessment until it becomes *just the way we do business* in both higher education and in workplace training programs?** Throughout this book, we will be answering this question from the perspective of four major factors that have the greatest influence on sustaining the work:

1. consistent leadership over time
2. instructor involvement from the *get-go*
3. professional development for staff and administrators
4. systems integration to ensure continuity

To say that these are the factors that have the greatest influence on sustainability is also to say that the lack of any of these factors is an important concern for sustaining this effort.

Our intent of PART ONE, then, is to provide you with some visual tools that will help you see the systemic nature of outcomes and assessment and how learning evidence can be used to renew and improve learning experiences over time.

In PART TWO, we provide you with four tools you can use to gauge the degree to which your organization's learning outcomes and assessment efforts are sustainable over time. Inherent in the design of these tools are four specific factors that are essential for sustaining outcome-based curricula. The tools are designed to help you make decisions about where your efforts need to be concentrated and set priorities for how you might use the rest of this Primer.

PARTS THREE, FOUR, FIVE and SIX provide scenarios and ideas for addressing the four major factors that will foster and sustain the flow of evidence in your organization: effective leadership, instructor involvement, professional development, and systems integration.

PART SEVEN evolved out of our research on leadership. That research convinced us that *TRUST* is so important to sustaining this work over time, that we needed to address it separately, not only as the final part of this Primer but also as the final part of the entire series.

Finally, as the capstone work of *The Outcome Primers Series 2.0*, this *Primer* stands on the shoulders of the other five Primers in that it requires an understanding of the major concepts developed there. For this reason, where needed, we briefly introduce a specific concept, but direct you to other Primers in this series for a fuller explanation.

Setting the Scene

Here are a couple of typical scenarios we hear about every day that relate to one or more of the four major factors we noted above that have the greatest influence on sustaining this work.

Scenario: A curriculum director in a large metropolitan college was an early believer in the power of creating program maps (see The MAPPING Primer: Mapping the Way to Learning Outcomes*) as a vehicle for helping everyone see how courses and assessment tasks align with intended learning outcomes. Guidelines for mapping a program call for the involvement of instructors, which can be messy and time-consuming. So, for efficiency's sake, she asked her administrative assistant to go ahead and create digital maps of all degree and certificate programs from what was already in the college catalogue. She wanted to streamline the process, creating each map quickly without involving faculty. Later she said, "Boy, was I wrong!"*

When they presented the beautifully digitized maps to the instructors and tried their best to generate a deep discussion, the instructors showed little interest in the image that was created of their program. It was then that they realized the mistake they had made. There is a reason instructors need to create and own their maps; it is their engagement in creating the map that drives the conversation and raises the questions that lead to program improvement.

This scenario illustrates the importance of instructor involvement from the *get-go* as a key factor in the sustainability of an outcomes and assessment effort.

We will admit that failing to involve instructors isn't the only mistake we make; it is usually not just one thing, but a combination of things, that hinder the outcomes and assessment effort. Here is another example.

Scenario: At a state university in California, the administration appointed one faculty member as coordinator of outcomes and assessment for the college, while appointing a different person to be in charge of faculty development for the college. For this college, it was seen as a big step forward.

The problem arose when the Chief Academic Officer instructed the person responsible for faculty development to host a session on assessment, and the person responsible for assessment learned of it through an email just three days prior to the event. At first, it seemed just an oversight which could be easily resolved, until the Chief Academic Officer acted alone to contract with a speaker whose message about assessment was contrary to what was being implemented in-house.

In this case, there were two leadership issues: lack of communication between leaders, and unclear role descriptions—both of which could have easily been avoided through better planning and understanding.

The above two scenarios paint a very small picture of the various kinds of issues we will address in this Primer. But in order to do that, we need to first be certain that we have a clear mental image of what it is that we are trying to sustain. What does a sustained flow of evidence look like? What role does the flow of learning evidence play in sustaining an outcomes and assessment system?

Learning Evidence

Definitions:

Learning evidence: *Qualitative and quantitative data that directly (e.g. projects, portfolios, tests) and indirectly (e.g. surveys, checklists, questionnaires) reflect learner achievement of intended learning outcomes.*

The flow of learning evidence: *The sustained process of gathering, tracking, reporting, analyzing and using learning evidence (examples above) for the expressed purpose of improving instructional programs and practices.*

Creating and sustaining a *flow of learning evidence* in any kind of educational organization is a complex task that requires a level of *systems thinking* that few of us developed in our graduate programs. As a result, it is difficult for most of us to even envision what a *flow of learning evidence* might look like across an organization. Where does it start? Where does it go? What feeds it? What stops it? How do we keep it flowing?

The answers to these questions are complicated by the fact that *learning evidence* flows at three different levels in any educational enterprise: organization, program, and course. It can be quite confusing when we lack a clear picture of how the levels interconnect.

Envisioning Everything in the Context of the Learner's Journey

When we subscribe to an outcome-based learning model, our first commitment is to assist learners on their journey toward learning outcomes that are pertinent to the real-life roles they are pursuing (e.g., worker, family member, community member, global citizen, lifelong learner, steward of the environment).

Throughout this entire Primer Series, the picture we paint of a learner's journey is one of paddlers in a large raft on a whitewater river with a guide at the back. Everyone has a paddle.

Starting by putting the raft into the river, the novice paddlers head down-river, learning as they go, navigating through increasingly difficult rapids until they are able to demonstrate all they have learned in a capstone (final) rapid, just prior to the take-out. This image is painted in Figure 1: The Learner's Journey, on pages 8–9.

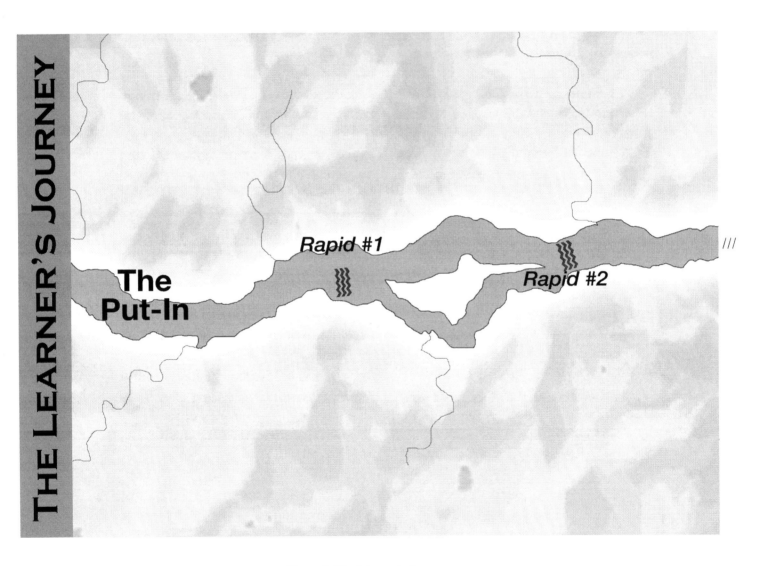

Figure 1: The Learner's Journey

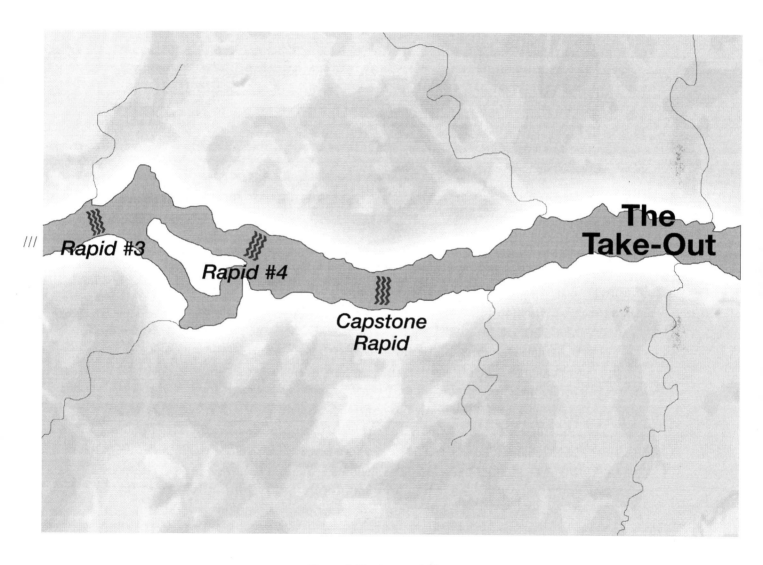

Figure 1: The Learner's Journey

In the same way that a river gathers more water as it flows to the sea, learners gather new skills and greater conceptual understanding as they move through new learning experiences. While there are many significant things the river metaphor helps us understand about learning, here are two that are especially pertinent to sustainability: 1) The essence of learning is a process of gathering, assessing, and integrating new concepts into what we have previously learned, and 2) like a river, learning doesn't stop—it might be dammed, but in a natural state, it never totally stops; even in the end, it recycles and continues to bring life to all things.

Let's continue with this metaphor. On the river, paddlers continuously learn new skills while avoiding obstacles and running the rapids where they show evidence of what they have learned. In the face-to-face or online classroom, learners also work to avoid obstacles and show evidence along the way through papers, presentations, demonstrations, and tests. On both the river and in the classroom, there is usually a culminating assessment task where evidence of the intended outcome is gathered, tracked, and used for purposes of advancing the learner and improving the learning experience.

Starting at Ground Zero— the Program Comes First

When we look at the learner's journey in the larger context of a program (rather than a course), what we see is an organized set of courses that is driven by several program outcomes, as illustrated in Figure 2: Ground Zero— The Program, on page 11.

Whether it be a degree, certification, or training program in a college, agency, or industry, each of these programs is composed of set of learning experiences—a dynamic interactive system. Since it is always best to begin with the larger picture, it is best to begin designing curriculum at the program

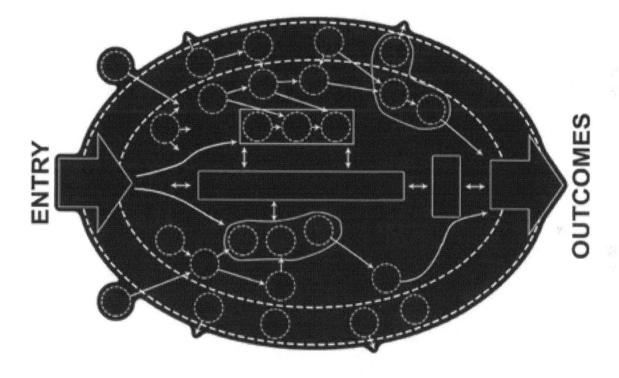

The PROGRAM
(Ground-Zero)

Figure 2: Ground Zero—The Program

level before *zooming in* on courses and workshops which are represented by the smaller circles in Figure 2. There are a lot of reasons why we consider the program as Ground Zero.

Try this:

Take a scrap piece of paper (or Post-it® Note) and tear a hole in the middle of the paper the diameter of your thumb. See Figure 3, below.

Now, hold it close to one eye with the other eye closed, and look at Figure

2 again. You should see the entire image through the hole.

Next, *zoom in* on the image by extending your arm to its full length until you see only a small isolated part of the whole—just one tiny part, while everything else is blocked by the paper. *Zoom in* tightly on one circle (representative of one course), and then *zoom back* to see the whole context.

It is easy to get lost in the processes of curriculum development. Are we looking at outcomes at the organization level, course level, or program level? It can all get so confusing. So, one of the keys to systems thinking is this ability to zoom *in and* zoom *back*. *Zoom in* to see processes; *zoom back* to see the larger system. When does *zooming* stop? It doesn't.

Now look more closely at an actual program map portrayed in Figure 4: Alternative Energy Degree Program Map, on pages 14 and 15. Notice that in this illustration of a program map, there are both linear and non-linear relationships

Figure 3: Zoomer

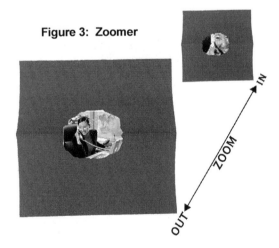

between courses/workshops (the circles on the map) that function together to achieve the intended program level outcomes. While these relationships are illustrated by different conventions for different kinds of programs, there are three things that are certain on a program map:

1) no course exists by itself in isolation,

2) all courses contribute to the program outcomes (or they no longer have a place in this program), and

3) evidence of both program outcomes and organization-wide outcomes flows from courses that make up the program.

In our view, the basic building block is the **program**. It's not an academic department, nor the training department. Learners don't navigate through departments; departments are the way we structure organizations. What the learner signs up for is a **PROGRAM** of

experiences and it is ground-zero for outcomes and assessment planning.

We have used the river metaphor here for only a specific purpose. For a broader look at how we use the river analogy, see The GUIDING Primer: Guiding Toward Learning Outcomes, The MAPPING Primer: Mapping the Way to Intended Outcomes, *and* The ASSESSMENT Primer: Assessing and Tracking Evidence of Learning Outcomes.

Alternative Energy Degree Program Map

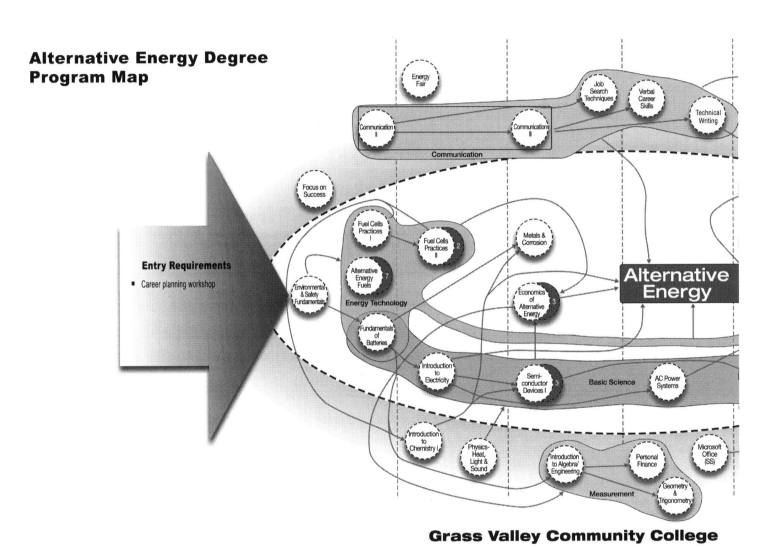

Figure 4: Alternative Energy Degree Program Map

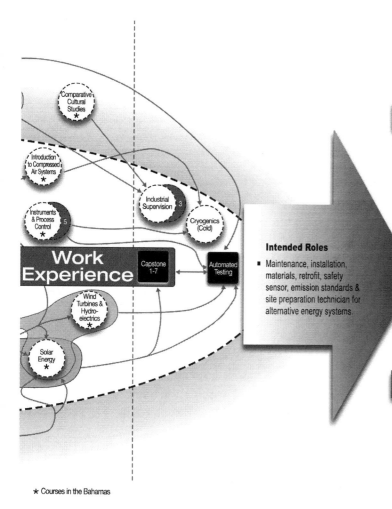

★ Courses in the Bahamas

Intended Roles

- Maintenance, installation, materials, retrofit, safety sensor, emission standards & site preparation technician for alternative energy systems.

INTENDED LEARNING OUTCOMES

1. Demonstrate effective verbal and written communication skills as an individual and as a team member.

2. Demonstrate basic electrical, mechanical, chemical, mathematical and computer skills involved in maintaining alternative energy systems.

3. Apply sound business and economic principles to achieve and maintain profitability of alternative energy systems.

4. Follow quality and safety procedures.

5. Install, repair and design alternative energy systems.

6. Fabricate and test prototypes.

7. Participate in researching current and emerging alternative energy systems.

ORGANIZATION-WIDE LEARNING OUTCOMES

- Communicate effectively
- Think critically
- Practice from a code of ethics
- Interact well with others
- Show evidence of cultural and global awareness

Thinking in Cycles

Putting these previous images of the learner's journey and program map aside for just a minute, there is a third image that will help complete the whole picture for us. It's the image depicted here in Figure 5.

Figure 5

Perhaps you have already noticed that we didn't bother to add a title to this figure. So, what title would you give it? Whirlwind? Cyclone? DVD? Recycling? Waterspout? Political spin? Washing machine? Kitchen blender? Solar system?

How about a pattern so wide-flung that it appears throughout the spectrum of reality: clouds, rivers, plants, cells, organisms, ecosystems, social systems, politics, influence, learning. It's the very pattern that sustains every form of life on earth as we know it.

To many of us, this image looks rather chaotic when compared to the earlier images we have seen in this Primer. The fact is we have a proclivity in western society for linearity. We expect to see linear patterns in almost everything. Take for example, the stock market where small investors react quickly to ups and downs with little thought for cycles—which would serve them much better. Or, consider how water flows in a seemingly straight line from a kitchen faucet to the drain in the sink. We don't often think big enough to see that in actuality, it is part of the world's river system that continuously recycles.

While we typically see learning as linear, the image of learning being cyclical is seldom envisioned. Let's discuss this in more detail in the following section.

Envisioning the Flow of Learning Evidence Across Time

Now that we have four images to work with (the river as learner's journey, the program, courses, and cycles), we can begin to envision how the continual flow of learning evidence leads to improving the quality of the experiences we offer learners.

Take a careful look at Figure 6, Program Level Self-Adjustment, on page 19. When we *zoom back* and see the entire learner's journey through a program, we see how evidence of program level learning outcomes can be collected throughout the program in designated courses. These critical assessment points are usually designated on a Program Map.

(You can see a Program Map at *www .outcomeprimers.com*). Evidence of learning that is collected at strategic points in the program is synthesized, analyzed, displayed and used to make decisions on where improvements need to be made as new learners are admitted to the program.

Figure 7, Course Level Self-Adjustment, on page 20, illustrates the same kind of flow pattern we see when we *zoom in* to the course level. At the end of every course, within an outcomes and assessment system, *evidence* of the intended outcomes is gathered and used to make adjustments in courses to improve learning. Both Figures 6 and 7 illustrate how the *flow of learning evidence* is a combination of both linear and cyclical thinking—the kind of thinking that leads to sustainability in every kind of system imaginable.

Figures 8 and 9, Flow of Learning Evidence at the Program and Course Levels respectively, pages 21 and 22, illustrate the iteration of the same self-adjustment pattern, over time, as both programs and courses get better and better at assisting learners in building proficiencies that are essential for the life-roles they anticipate.

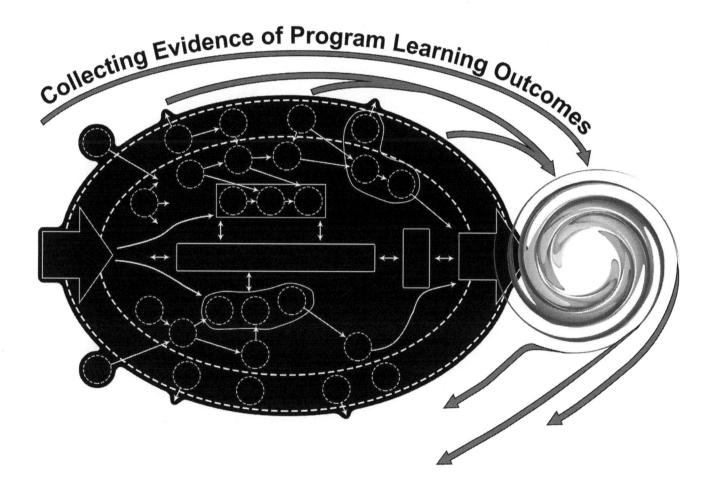

Figure 6: Program Level Self-Adjustment

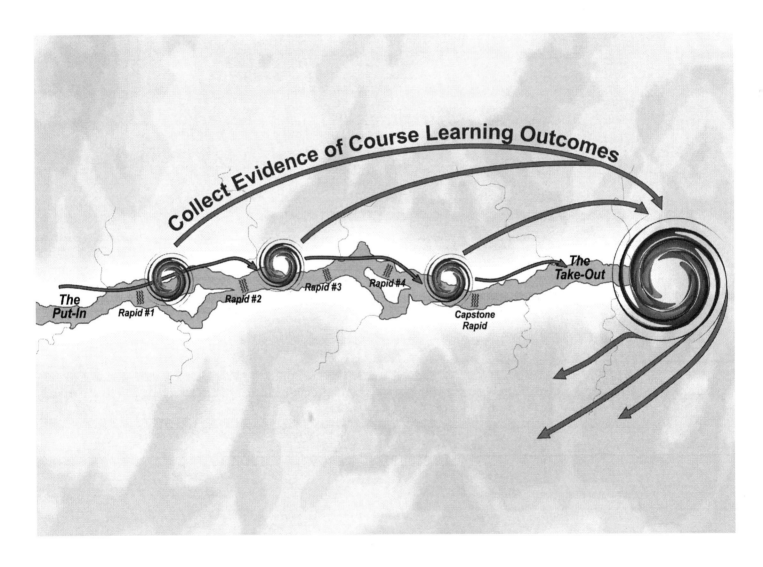

Figure 7: Course Level Self-Adjustment

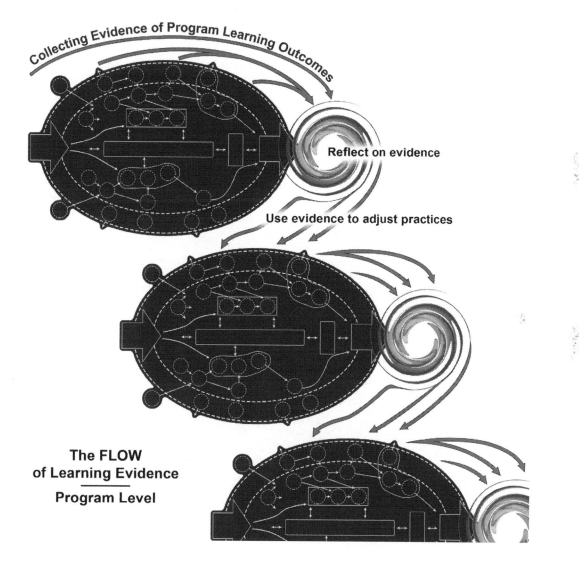

Collecting Evidence of Program Learning Outcomes

Reflect on evidence

Use evidence to adjust practices

The FLOW
of Learning Evidence
———
Program Level

Figure 8: Flow of Learning Evidence at the Program Level

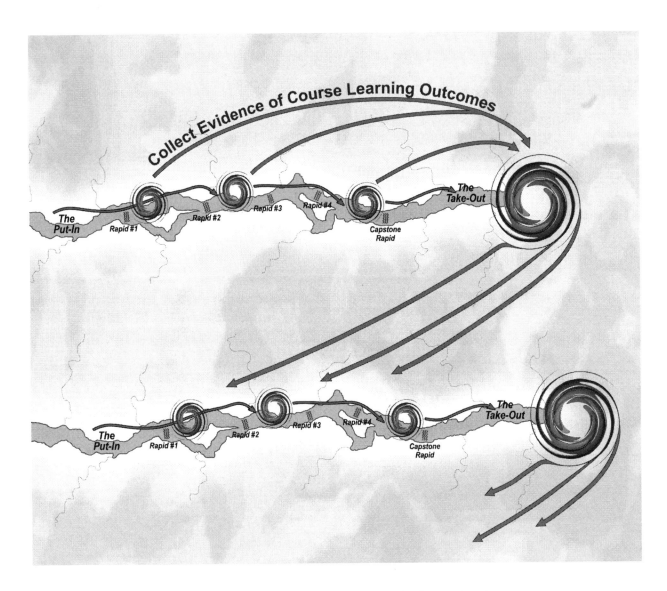

Figure 9: Flow of Learning Evidence at the Course Level

Summary

Struggling to comply with imposed standards by outside agencies might not be the best way to build sustainable academic or training programs. There are better reasons, like caring enough to self-adjust our practices based on real evidence of learning. However, accrediting agencies have done a great deal to initiate constructive learning experiences for colleges, including a particular focus on their system for learning outcomes and assessment.

In PART ONE, we have drawn on two universal flow patterns to help us grasp a better understanding of the *forward journey of the learner* and the *recycling nature of self-adjustment.* We have shown how the patterns repeat themselves across different levels of the curriculum.

Of special note has been the designation of the PROGRAM as the best place to begin thinking about learning outcomes and assessment. All outcomes connect and align within the *program*—course outcomes, workshop outcomes, seminar outcomes, internship outcomes, and even organization-wide outcomes. By looking first at the program level, then *zooming back* to the organization and *zooming in* to courses and workshops, we are able to make decisions that sustain the whole system. In addition, beginning our planning at the program level discourages a proliferation of courses and instead, promotes retention and program completion, two of the major challenges in adult education today.

PART TWO

Gauging The Sustainability of an Outcomes and Assessment System

It's when something works that people take their eyes off it.

—Barbara Bessey

Introduction

In PART TWO, we provide you with four tools you can use to gauge the degree to which your organization's learning outcomes and assessment design efforts are sustainable over time. Inherent in the design of these tools are four specific factors that are essential for sustaining an outcomes and assessment system. The tools are designed to help you make decisions about where your efforts need to be concentrated and set priorities for how you might use the rest of this Primer.

We begin here with the assumption that your organization already has in place some kind of system for establishing and assessing learning outcomes. We also assume that it is a work in progress and not in a static state (or at least, we hope not).

It's possible that some of you are struggling along and could use this series of Primers to improve the system you are trying to create, while others have a system in place that seems to be working well. In both cases, we have written PART TWO for you. If you are still struggling—we will help you see where to put your energies. But, if your system is up and working, these next pages are particularly important because *it's when things work that we tend to take our eyes off them, and systems fall apart.*

Four Critical Factors in Sustaining an Outcomes and Assessment System

Based on our own work in (and with) colleges and educational agencies across the USA and Canada, we have identified four major factors that directly and indirectly affect the sustainability of outcomes and assessment systems wherever they are initiated: 1) leadership, 2) instructor involvement, 3) professional development, and 4) system integration. The identification of these four major factors is further supported by Gilbert's

(1996) research on behavior engineering and Binder's (1998) adaptation of his Six Boxes Model which are both based on over 60 years of basic behavior science.

In examining the literature of human performance improvement and high performance organizations, we looked for models and characteristics suggested by the people who are actually engaged in sustaining the outcomes and assessment initiatives in organizations. Though the models we drew from were used to examine an existing system, it appeared to us that they were just as useful to those who were just beginning to build a system.

For each of the four factors that make up the Sustainability Tools on these next several pages, we have identified numerous indicators that give depth and definition to each factor. As we developed the specific indicators for each respective factor, we drew from the literature on systems thinking including relational characteristics of sustainable systems, alignment, flow, emergence, self-organization, self-adjustment, cycles, feedback loops, and resilience.

The interesting thing about these four factors and their respective indicators is that they play out in slightly different ways at four different system levels: organization-wide, program, course, and instructor. For this reason, we created separate tools (with similar but different questions) for each level of the curriculum. Here is an overview of the factors that make up each of the sustainability tools.

Leadership—An Overview

Of the four different factors, leadership (or lack of it) is usually the variable that has the greatest effect on the sustainability of an outcome and assessment system. And when we talk about leadership, we mean leadership at different levels and positions in the organization: the college-wide academic officer, the college-wide assessment coordinator, the program leader or coordinator, the curriculum and assessment committee members, the faculty members who coordinate multiple sections of one course, and the instructors who guide learners. Leadership is a shared and decentralized responsibility in an outcomes and assessment system.

Effective leadership involves many different things at each of these different levels, and any time there is a change in leadership, there is a natural disruption. That's why it is important to have both a succession and a transition plan in place at each level of leadership.

In the year 2015 alone, community colleges experienced 269 turn-overs in presidencies, which means that nearly one in four community colleges experienced a transition at the highest level of leadership. As of July 2016, Ashley Smith reported on the website *Inside Higher Education* that there had already been 203 turn-overs in community college leadership. The real significance of this data is that when there is change at the very top, there are usually subse-quent changes that ripple through other leadership positions that have a direct effect on whether an outcomes and assessment initiative is sustained. And by the way, one of the biggest challenges we have is how little some top-level administrators know, or care about, learning outcomes and assessment.

To assure that a college or university has organization-wide support for learning outcomes and assessment efforts, many colleges have created new positions for outcomes and assessment coordinators. This is evidenced by the high number of job openings posted on a list-serve sponsored by the Association for the Assessment of Learning in Higher Education (2016). It's a good sign.

Instructor Involvement—An Overview

When we express a concern about good leadership in outcomes and assessment, we are in no way suggesting that administrative leaders are the ones who get the whole job done. While administrative leadership is important, it's always the classroom instructor who, in the end, *guides learners*, *delivers the goods*, and *collects the evidence of learning*.

When leaders lay out all the plans for outcomes and assessment, instructors rarely buy in. On the other hand, when they are involved in creating outcomes and assessment tools, they are far more likely to integrate outcomes and assessment in their classrooms, which in the end, is what really counts.

To make the system sustainable, every instructor involved with guiding learners needs to be given the opportunity for professional development in the area of outcomes and assessment. And, to the fullest extent possible, they need to be involved in improving assessment instruments, policies that directly affect learner success, and the system itself. Perhaps the ultimate kind of involvement is when instructors help each other, and share new ideas and practices

that improve learning outcomes and assessment. Any time we co-create, we inherently build trust, which is essential to this work.

Professional Development— An Overview

As outcomes and assessment systems evolve, they take on their own language and become an area of professional specialization. This is good, except that instructors are primarily hired for their subject matter expertise, academic degrees, and traditional teaching experience, not their preparation in learning outcomes and assessment.

The assumption throughout higher education has always been that if people have in-depth knowledge in a subject area, they can develop a curriculum and teach it. But all of this comes into question when we create a learning outcomes and assessment system based on life-roles and develop assessment tools that reflect real-life outcomes instead of a defined body of knowledge.

What this means is that even for experienced instructors, professional development opportunities are essential to the sustainability of the outcomes and assessment effort.

The most advanced organizations have in-house professional development that assures all administrators and instructors are knowledgeable about learning outcomes and assessment in addition to their subject expertise. As a result, all instructors are engaged collaboratively with administration. Here is just a sample of some of the basic things all administrators and instructors should be able to do given the right professional development opportunities:

- create, interpret and align course outcomes with program and organization-wide outcomes,

- create and align learning activities and assessment tasks with learning outcomes,

- define essential concepts, skills and issues needed to meet the intended learning outcomes,

- adjust, create, and use assessment tools (rubrics, scoring guides, surveys, etc.),

- derive quantitative data from qualitative evidence,

- analyze and use the results of learning assessment to improve courses and programs,

- help learners build proficiencies that are relevant to the intended learning outcomes and life-roles, and

- communicate with learners and other instructors using accurate and consistent terminology related to learning outcomes and assessment.

Most of the above skills relate to curricular design in addition to an instructor's ability to guide (teach). A more complete list is shown in PART FIVE.

System Integration—An Overview

Curricular work in colleges is most often carried out by a series of separate committees and/or departments serving four seemingly different purposes: 1) Curriculum—oversee curriculum design and approval, 2) Assessment—oversee learning assessment at the program, organization, and course level, 3) Program Review—oversee program review, and 4) Professional Development—plan and deliver professional development opportunities for the faculty and staff. But in order to function as an effective system, attention has to be given to the inputs, outputs, and feedback loops that connect them to each other—an Outcomes and Assessment System. As in all systems, the work takes on a collaborative nature. If one part is not working well, it affects all the other parts.

System integration is the one factor that we seem to know the least about and see the least evidence of in outcomes and assessment systems. There is much for us to learn.

Four Sustainability Tools

What is a Sustainability Tool?

A Sustainability Tool is a set of specific questions pertaining to the four critical factors that influence the sustainability of a learning outcomes and assessment system.

What is the purpose of a Sustainability Tool?

The purpose of the Sustainability Tools is to assess the degree to which four factors (leadership, instructor involvement, professional development, and system integration) are impacting the sustainability of a learning outcomes and assessment initiative. We know the pain that comes with working hard to develop a system only to find it severely lacking, or even dismantled over time. The Sustainability Tools are designed to help you assess how these factors are *playing out* in your own college.

Suggestions For Using These Tools

Persons at different levels of the organization will use the Sustainability Tools, as shown on pages 35–50, in different ways. Here are some options:

Academic Officers (Use all tools.)

1) Consider using all the tools across the organization to get a glimpse of the current state of the institution's outcome and assessment system.

2) Use the tools to determine priorities and set realistic expectations for professional development efforts.

3) Use sections of each tool independently. For example, extract the leadership section and use it separately at one or all levels.

4) Use the tools to focus a group or committee discussion around outcomes and assessment at any or all levels of the system.

Program Coordinators/Managers and Advisory Committees (Use program level tool.)

1) Use the program-level tool to focus a discussion with your advisory committee about learning outcomes and assessment.

2) Extract a specific section (or one question) from the tool to focus the conversation in a program meeting.

3) Use the tool to gather data that will help set priorities for professional development and the use of external resources.

4) Use the tool to help your team articulate your needs for support from top management.

5) When appropriate, use the tool as part of your self-review in preparation for an accreditation visit or certification by an external agency.

Lead Instructors (Use course-level tool.)

1) Use the course-level tool to discuss outcomes and assessment as it relates to a specific course.

2) Extract and use a specific section (or one question) from the tool to help identify where improvements can be made.

3) Use the tool to help articulate your needs for support.

Individual Instructors (Use the instructor-level tool.)

1) Use the instructor-level tool to examine each course you teach for alignment between outcomes, assessment tasks, content, learning activities, and learning evidence.

2) Use the tool to initiate discussion with instructors who teach courses that connect with yours.

The questions on each of the Sustainability Tools are meant to prompt dialogue, shared discovery, and coordinated planning—things that are essential to any system. Each of the tools we have included in this series of Primers help to make the "whole" system visible to all of us, whether we are administrators, stakeholders, staff, or instructors.

Sustainability Tool: Organization-wide Level

Use this rating scale when assessing each indicator under the 4 critical factors.
Y – yes, done consistently   N – No, not on radar   NI – needs improvement

Purpose of this tool:	To provide a systems and an appreciative inquiry approach to examining the effectiveness and sustainability of the organization-wide learning outcome and assessment process. The results will determine any next steps that will improve and sustain the flow of learning evidence.
Who should use this tool?	Assessment committee, assessment professionals, institutional research professionals.
How do you use this tool?	Use as a discussion guide, focusing on each of the four factors—one at a time. Involve those who can answer the questions best to ensure accurate information. Carefully document strengths found and improvements needed. Put together a short-term (one year) and long-term (3–5 years) action plan.
When do you use this tool?	• As a starting point to get baseline information for reporting to internal and external stakeholders. • When there are issues with the process and you want to look at contributing factors. • On an annual basis, to review the status, celebrate progress, and determine next steps.

Leadership	Y	N	NI	Notes
1. Is there a champion that is responsible for setting expectations and determining priorities about organization-wide learning outcomes and assessment?	☐	☐	☐	
2. Is there a committee/department that is responsible for creating, refining, and reviewing organization-wide learning outcomes, their assessment and related processes?	☐	☐	☐	
3. Is there a succession and transition plan in place for the champion and committee/department leadership that assures the continuation of the organization-wide learning outcomes and assessment plan?	☐	☐	☐	
4. Are the champion and committee/department able to share an organization-wide learning outcomes and assessment vision with instructors and stakeholders so everyone has a shared meaning?	☐	☐	☐	
5. Do the champion and committee/department involve all instructors in organization-wide outcome and assessment decisions?	☐	☐	☐	

Figure 10: Sustainability Tool—Organization-wide Level, 1 of 5

Sustainability Tool: Organization-wide Level				
Use this rating scale when assessing each indicator under the 4 critical factors. Y – yes, done consistently N – No, not on radar NI – needs improvement				
6. Do the champion and committee/department systematically review organization-wide learning outcomes and evidence of learning as well as related design documents? See *The OUTCOME Primer: Envisioning Learning Outcomes*, *The CONTENT Primer: Aligning Essential Content with Learning Outcomes*, and *The MAPPING Primer: Mapping the Way to Learning Outcomes* for design documents.	☐	☐	☐	
7. Do the champion, committee/department, and college administration provide support necessary for the instructors and staff to sustain a flow of learning evidence over time (i.e. curriculum design and assessment, documentation, technology, and allocation of time)?	☐	☐	☐	
8. Do the champion and committee/departments recognize, value, and celebrate the efforts of instructors and staff to gather, track, and use learning evidence to improve organization-wide learning outcomes?	☐	☐	☐	
9. Do the champion and committee/department foster trust by being consistent, reliable, respectful, and accountable for organization-wide learning outcomes?	☐	☐	☐	
Instructor Involvement	**Y**	**N**	**NI**	**Notes**
1. Are instructors and committee/department roles and responsibilities for organization-wide learning outcomes and assessment documented and understood by all instructors?	☐	☐	☐	
2. Do instructors take advantage of professional development opportunities to build their proficiency in developing, assessing, and guiding outcome-based learning?	☐	☐	☐	
3. Are instructors included when developing and revising organization-wide learning outcomes that all graduates must exhibit?	☐	☐	☐	
4. Are instructors included when developing and revising organization-wide learning outcome assessment plans as well as the criteria and standards to be measured?	☐	☐	☐	

Figure 10: Sustainability Tool—Organization-wide Level, 2 of 5

Sustainability Tool: Organization-wide Level				
Use this rating scale when assessing each indicator under the 4 critical factors. Y – yes, done consistently N – No, not on radar NI – needs improvement				
5. Are instructors involved in determining and documenting which organization-wide learning outcomes align best with the courses they teach?	☐	☐	☐	
6. Do the committee/department and instructors openly discuss learning evidence and make data-informed decisions about organization-wide learning outcomes and assessment?	☐	☐	☐	
7. Are instructors involved in developing and improving assessment criteria, instruments, processes, policy, and culture related to organization-wide learning outcomes and assessment?	☐	☐	☐	
8. Are instructors involved in assessing learners' work (i.e. learning artifacts)?	☐	☐	☐	
9. Do instructors interact and assist each other in assuring the flow of learning evidence for organization-wide learning outcomes and assessment?	☐	☐	☐	
10. Are instructors made aware of learner performance in meeting organization-wide learning outcomes and involved in the discussion of potential changes based on that evidence?	☐	☐	☐	
11. Do instructors foster trust by being consistent, reliable, respectful, and accountable for organization-wide learning outcomes and assessment?	☐	☐	☐	
Professional Development	**Y**	**N**	**NI**	**Notes**
1. Do the committee/department and instructors interpret the organization-wide learning outcomes the same way and know how to integrate and align them with their programs and courses?	☐	☐	☐	
2. Can all instructors who teach courses that align with one or more organization-wide learning outcome(s) articulate how these outcomes are relevant for real-life roles?	☐	☐	☐	

Figure 10: Sustainability Tool—Organization-wide Level, 3 of 5

Sustainability Tool: Organization-wide Level			
Use this rating scale when assessing each indicator under the 4 critical factors. Y – yes, done consistently N – No, not on radar NI – needs improvement			
3. Can all instructors create institutional documents and other design documents that show the alignment of outcomes? See *The OUTCOME Primer: Envisioning Learning Outcomes* and *The CONTENT Primer: Aligning Essential Content with Learning Outcomes* to learn how to create a COG (Course Outcome Guide) that aligns with a POG (Program Outcome Guide).	☐	☐	☐
4. Can all instructors align their course learning outcomes with the organization-wide learning outcomes and other courses for which their course functions as a prerequisite?	☐	☐	☐
5. Can all instructors create and align learning experiences with organization-wide learning outcomes?	☐	☐	☐
6. Can all instructors guide learners and provide effective feedback to support the achievement of learning outcomes?	☐	☐	☐
7. Can all instructors adjust, create, or use assessment tools (rubrics, scoring guides, checklists, surveys) that align with the organization-wide learning outcomes?	☐	☐	☐
8. Can all instructors assess learners' work (i.e. artifacts) using an assessment tool that aligns with organization-wide learning outcomes?	☐	☐	☐
9. Can all instructors generate, analyze, and use organization-wide learning evidence to determine and document how best to adjust and improve learning?	☐	☐	☐
10. Are organization-wide learning outcome and assessment skills and abilities acknowledged and supported?	☐	☐	☐

Figure 10: Sustainability Tool—Organization-wide Level, 4 of 5

Sustainability Tool: Organization-wide Level

Use this rating scale when assessing each indicator under the 4 critical factors.
Y – yes, done consistently   N – No, not on radar   NI – needs improvement

System Integration	Y	N	NI	Notes
1. Is there a common language used when talking about curricular and an organization-wide outcomes and assessment processes?	☐	☐	☐	
2. Is there alignment between course, program, and organization-wide outcomes?	☐	☐	☐	
3. Is the process for organization-wide outcome and assessment well defined, documented, and followed?	☐	☐	☐	
4. Are the roles and responsibilities of those involved with organization-wide learning outcomes and assessment documented, understood, and followed?	☐	☐	☐	
5. Are committees and the departments that are involved in related processes, communicating, collaborating, and coordinating their efforts to ensure integration and efficiency?	☐	☐	☐	
6. Are the organization-wide learning outcomes and assessment process, methods, and tools documented, centrally located, readily accessible, consistently used, and routinely updated?	☐	☐	☐	
7. Is technology carefully selected and used to enhance consistency and efficiency?	☐	☐	☐	
8. Is the organization-wide learning outcomes and assessment process integrated with related processes such as curriculum design, learning assessment, and program review?	☐	☐	☐	
9. Is there a plan and process to review and update organization-wide learning outcomes and related processes on a regular basis to make needed adjustments?	☐	☐	☐	
10. Is organization-wide learning data used only for its intended purpose and shared with all stakeholders?	☐	☐	☐	

Figure 10: Sustainability Tool—Organization-wide Level, 5 of 5

Sustainability Tool: Program Level

Use this rating scale when assessing each indicator under the 4 critical factors.
Y – yes, done consistently   N – No, not on radar   NI – needs improvement

Purpose of this tool:	To provide a systems and an appreciative inquiry approach to examining the effectiveness and sustainability of the program learning outcome and assessment process. The results will determine any next steps that will improve and sustain the flow of learning evidence. NOTE: This tool supports and integrates with a Program Quality Management System approach.
Who should use this tool?	Program coordinators, instructional staff, and advisory groups.
How do you use this tool?	Use as a discussion guide, focusing on each of the four factors—one at a time. Involve those who can answer the questions best to ensure accurate information. Carefully document strengths found and improvements needed. Put together a short-term (one year) and long-term (3–5 years) action plan.
When do you use this tool?	• As a starting point to get baseline information for reporting to internal and external stakeholders. • When there are issues with the process and you want to look at contributing factors. • On an annual basis, to review the status, celebrate progress, and determine next steps.

Leadership	Y	N	NI	Notes
1. Is the program coordinator(s) a champion of outcome-based learning and assessment?	☐	☐	☐	
2. Is there a succession and transition plan for the program?	☐	☐	☐	
3. Is the program coordinator able to share the outcomes and assessment vision with instructors and stakeholders so everyone has a shared meaning?	☐	☐	☐	
4. Does the program coordinator involve all instructors in program outcomes and assessment decisions?	☐	☐	☐	
5. Does the advisory group have representative(s) from organizations that could hire the graduates of this program?	☐	☐	☐	
6. Do the program coordinator, advisory committee, and other stakeholders systematically review the program's learning outcomes and evidence of learning as well as related design documents? See *The OUTCOME Primer: Envisioning Learning Outcomes*, *The CONTENT Primer: Aligning Essential Content with Learning Outcomes*, and *The MAPPING Primer: Mapping the Way to Learning Outcomes* for design documents.	☐	☐	☐	

Figure 11: Sustainability Tool—Program Level, 1 of 5

Sustainability Tool: Program Level				
Use this rating scale when assessing each indicator under the 4 critical factors. Y – yes, done consistently N – No, not on radar NI – needs improvement				
7. Do the program coordinator and college administration provide the support necessary for the instructors and staff to sustain a flow of program learning evidence over time (i.e. curriculum design and assessment, documentation, technology, and allocation of time)?	☐	☐	☐	
8. Does the program coordinator recognize, value, and celebrate the efforts of instructors and staff to gather, track, and use program learning evidence to improve the program?	☐	☐	☐	
9. Does the program coordinator foster trust by being consistent, reliable, respectful, and accountable for program outcomes and assessment?	☐	☐	☐	
Instructor Involvement	Y	N	NI	**Notes**
1. Are program instructor and related committee/department roles and responsibilities for program outcomes and assessment documented and understood by all instructors?	☐	☐	☐	
2. Do program instructors take advantage of professional development opportunities to build their proficiency in developing, assessing, and guiding outcome-based learning?	☐	☐	☐	
3. Are program instructors included when developing and revising program outcome statements that prepare graduates for real-life roles?	☐	☐	☐	
4. Are program instructors included when developing and revising program assessment plans as well as criteria and standards to be measured?	☐	☐	☐	
5. Do program instructors understand where their course fits in the learner's journey? Do they have appropriate program documentation (program maps, program sequence, program description, program outcomes, etc.)? See *The MAPPING Primer: Mapping the Way to Learning Outcomes*.	☐	☐	☐	
6. Do program coordinators and instructors openly discuss the program's learning evidence and make data-informed decisions about program changes?	☐	☐	☐	
7. Are program instructors involved in developing and improving program assessment criteria, instruments, processes, policy, and culture?	☐	☐	☐	
8. Are program instructors included in assessing learner's work (i.e. learning artifacts)?	☐	☐	☐	

Figure 11: Sustainability Tool—Program Level, 2 of 5

Sustainability Tool: Program Level

Use this rating scale when assessing each indicator under the 4 critical factors.
Y – yes, done consistently   N – No, not on radar   NI – needs improvement

	Y	N	NI	Notes
9. Do program instructors interact and assist each other in assuring the appropriate sequencing of the learner's journey as well as the flow of program learning evidence?	☐	☐	☐	
10. Are program instructors made aware of learner performance on end-of-program assessments and involved in the discussion of potential changes based on that evidence?	☐	☐	☐	
11. Do program instructors foster trust by being consistent, reliable, respectful, and accountable for program outcomes and assessment?	☐	☐	☐	
Professional Development	**Y**	**N**	**NI**	**Notes**
1. Do instructors in the program interpret the program learning outcomes the same way and know how their courses contribute to those outcomes?	☐	☐	☐	
2. Can all instructors who teach courses in this program (including general education) articulate how their course is relevant for learners in this program?	☐	☐	☐	
3. Can all instructors create institutional documents and other design documents that show the alignment of outcomes? See *The OUTCOME Primer: Envisioning Learning Outcomes* and *The CONTENT Primer: Aligning Essential Content with Learning Outcomes* to learn how to create a COG (Course Outcome Guide) that aligns with a POG (Program Outcome Guide).	☐	☐	☐	
4. Can all program instructors align their course learning outcomes with the program learning outcomes and other courses for which their course functions as a prerequisite?	☐	☐	☐	
5. Can all program instructors guide learners and provide effective feedback to support the achievement of the intended learning outcomes?	☐	☐	☐	
6. Can all program instructors create and align learnng experiences with program learning outcomes?	☐	☐	☐	

Figure 11: Sustainability Tool—Program Level, 3 of 5

Sustainability Tool: Program Level				
Use this rating scale when assessing each indicator under the 4 critical factors. Y – yes, done consistently N – No, not on radar NI – needs improvement				
7. Can all program instructors adjust, create, or use assessment tools (rubrics, scoring guides, checklists, surveys) that align with the program learning outcomes?	☐	☐	☐	
8. Can all program instructors assess a learner's work (i.e. artifacts) using an assessment instrument that aligns with program learning outcomes?	☐	☐	☐	
9. Can all program instructors generate, analyze, and use program learning evidence to determine and document how best to adjust and improve learning?	☐	☐	☐	
10. Are program learning outcomes and assessment skills and abilities acknowledged and supported?	☐	☐	☐	
System Integration	**Y**	**N**	**NI**	**Notes**
1. Is there a common language used when talking about curricular and program outcomes and assessment processes?	☐	☐	☐	
2. Is there alignment between course, program, and organization-wide outcomes?	☐	☐	☐	
3. Is the program outcomes and assessment process well defined, documented, and followed?	☐	☐	☐	
4. Are the roles and responsibilities of all stakeholders documented, understood, and followed?	☐	☐	☐	
5. Are committees and departments involved in related processes communicating, collaborating, and coordinating their efforts to ensure integration and efficiency?	☐	☐	☐	
6. Are the process, methods, and tools documented, centrally located, readily accessible, consistently used, and routinely updated?	☐	☐	☐	
7. Is technology carefully selected and used to enhance consistency and efficiency?	☐	☐	☐	

Figure 11: Sustainability Tool—Program Level, 4 of 5

Sustainability Tool: Program Level			
Use this rating scale when assessing each indicator under the 4 critical factors. Y – yes, done consistently N – No, not on radar NI – needs improvement			
8. Is the program outcomes and assessment process integrated with related processes such as organization-wide learning outcomes and assessment, program updates, program reviews?	☐ ☐ ☐	
9. Is there a plan and process to review and update the program outcomes and related processes on a regular basis to make needed adjustments?	☐ ☐ ☐	
10. Is program learning outcomes data used only for its intended purpose and shared with all stakeholders?	☐ ☐ ☐	

Figure 11: Sustainability Tool—Program Level, 5 of 5

Sustainability Tool: Course (Multi-Section) Level

Use this rating scale when assessing each indicator under the 4 critical factors.
Y – yes, done consistently   N – No, not on radar   NI – needs improvement

Purpose of this tool:	To provide a systems and an appreciative inquiry approach to examining the effectiveness and sustainability of the course learning outcome and assessment process for multi-sections. The results will determine any next steps that will improve and sustain the flow of learning evidence.
Who should use this tool?	Assessment professionals, institutional research, instructional staff.
How do you use this tool?	Use as a discussion guide, focusing on each of the four factors—one at a time. Involve those who can answer the questions best to ensure accurate information. Carefully document strengths found and improvements needed. Put together a short-term (one year) and long-term (3–5 years) action plan.
When do you use this tool?	• As a starting point to get baseline information for reporting to internal and external stakeholders. • When there are issues with the process and you want to look at contributing factors. • On an annual basis, to review the status, celebrate progress, and determine next steps.

Leadership	Y	N	NI	Notes
1. Is there a champion of multi-section course outcomes and assessment?	☐	☐	☐	
2. Is there a succession and transition plan for the champion that assures the continuation of the multi-section course outcomes and assessment plan?	☐	☐	☐	
3. Is the champion able to share the multi-section course outcomes and assessment vision with instructors and stakeholder so everyone has a shared meaning?	☐	☐	☐	
4. Does the champion involve all instructors in the multi-section course outcomes and assessment decisions?	☐	☐	☐	
5. Does the champion, any related committee/department, and instructors systematically review the course learning outcomes and learning evidence as well as related design documents? See *The OUTCOME Primer: Envisioning Learning Outcomes*, *The CONTENT Primer: Aligning Essential Content with Learning Outcomes*, and *The MAPPING Primer: Mapping the Way to Learning Outcomes* for design documents.	☐	☐	☐	
6. Do the champion and college administration provide the support necessary for the instructors and staff to sustain a flow of multi-section course learning evidence over time (i.e. curriculum design and assessment, documentation, technology, and allocation of time)?	☐	☐	☐	

Figure 12: Sustainability Tool—Course (Multi-Section) Level, 1 of 4

Sustainability Tool: Course (Multi-Section) Level

Use this rating scale when assessing each indicator under the 4 critical factors.
Y – yes, done consistently   N – No, not on radar   NI – needs improvement

	Y	N	NI	Notes
7. Does the champion recognize, value, and celebrate the efforts of instructors and staff to gather, track, and use multi-section course learning evidence to improve the course?	☐	☐	☐	
8. Does the champion foster trust by being consistent, reliable, respectful, and account-able for multi-section course outcome and assessment?	☐	☐	☐	
Instructor Involvement	**Y**	**N**	**NI**	**Notes**
1. Are course instructor and any committee/department roles and responsibilities for multi-section course outcomes and assessment documented and understood by all instructors?	☐	☐	☐	
2. Do course instructors take advantage of professional development opportunities to build their proficiency in developing, assessing, and guiding outcome-based learning?	☐	☐	☐	
3. Are course instructors included when developing and revising course outcome state-ments that align with real-life roles?	☐	☐	☐	
4. Are course instructors included when developing and revising multi-section course assessment plans as well as criteria and standards to be measured?	☐	☐	☐	
5. Do course instructors understand where their course fits in the learner's journey? Do they have appropriate course documentation (course outcome guides, program map, etc.)? Were they involved in developing these? See *The OUTCOME Primer: Envision-ing Learning Outcomes* and *The CONTENT Primer: Aligning Essential Content with Learning Outcomes* to learn how to create a COG (Course Outcome Guide) that aligns with a POG (Program Outcome Guide), *The MAPPING Primer: Mapping the Way to Learning Outcomes.*	☐	☐	☐	
6. Do the champion and instructors openly discuss course learning evidence and make data-informed decisions about course changes?	☐	☐	☐	
7. Are course instructors involved in developing and improving course assessment crite-ria, instruments, processes, policy, and culture?	☐	☐	☐	
8. Are course instructors included in assessing learners' work (i.e. learning artifacts)?	☐	☐	☐	
9. Do course instructors interact and assist each other in assuring the appropriate se-quencing of the learner's journey as well as the flow of course learning evidence?	☐	☐	☐	

Figure 12: Sustainability Tool—Course (Multi-Section) Level, 2 of 4

Sustainability Tool: Course (Multi-Section) Level

Use this rating scale when assessing each indicator under the 4 critical factors.
Y – yes, done consistently   N – No, not on radar   NI – needs improvement

	Y	N	NI	Notes
10. Are course instructors made aware of learner performance on capstone assessments and involved the the discussion of potential changes based on the evidence?	☐	☐	☐	
11. Do course instructors foster trust by being consistent, reliable, respectul, and accountable for course outcome and assessment?	☐	☐	☐	
Professional Development	Y	N	NI	**Notes**
1. Do instructors that teach the same course interpret the course learning outcomes in the same way and know how their course contributes to any higher-level outcomes (program or organization-wide)?	☐	☐	☐	
2. Can all instructors create institutional documents and other design documents that show the alignment of outcomes? See *The OUTCOME Primer: Envisioning Learning Outcomes* and *The CONTENT Primer: Aligning Essential Content with Learning Outcomes* to learn how to create a COG (Course Outcome Guide) that aligns with a POG (Program Outcome Guide).	☐	☐	☐	
3. Can course instructors align their course learning outcomes with related program learning outcomes and other courses for which their course functions as a prerequisite?	☐	☐	☐	
4. Can all course instructors create and align learning experiences with course learning outcomes?	☐	☐	☐	
5. Can all course instructors guide learners and provide effective feedback to support the achievement of the intended learning outcomes?	☐	☐	☐	
6. Can all course instructors adjust, create, or use assessment tools (rubrics, scoring guides, checklists, surveys) that align with the course learning outcomes?	☐	☐	☐	
7. Can all course instructors assess learners' work (i.e. learning artifacts) using an assessment instrument that aligns with the course learning outcomes?	☐	☐	☐	
8. Can all course instructors generate, analyze, and use learning evidence to determine and document how best to adjust and improve learning?	☐	☐	☐	
9. Are multi-section course learning outcome and assessment skills and abilities acknowledged and supported?	☐	☐	☐	

Figure 12: Sustainability Tool—Course (Multi-Section) Level, 3 of 4

Sustainability Tool: Course (Multi-Section) Level

Use this rating scale when assessing each indicator under the 4 critical factors.
Y – yes, done consistently   N – No, not on radar   NI – needs improvement

System Integration	Y	N	NI	Notes
1. Is there a common language used when talking about curricular processes and a multi-section course outcome and assessment process?	☐	☐	☐	
2. Is there alignment between course, program, and organization-wide outcomes?	☐	☐	☐	
3. Is the process for multi-section course outcomes and assessment well-defined, documented and followed?	☐	☐	☐	
4. Are the roles and responsibilities of all stakeholders documented, understood, and followed?	☐	☐	☐	
5. Are committees/departments, involved in related processes, communicating, collaborating, and coordinating their efforts to ensure integration and efficiency?	☐	☐	☐	
6. Is the multi-section course process, methods, and tools documented, centrally located, readily accessible, consistently used, and routinely updated?	☐	☐	☐	
7. Is technology carefully selected and used to enhance consistency and efficiency?	☐	☐	☐	
8. Is the process for multi-section course outcome and assessment integrated with related processes such as organization-wide learning outcome and assessment, course updates, and course review?	☐	☐	☐	
9. Is there a plan and process to review and update course outcomes and related processes on a regular basis to make needed adjustments?	☐	☐	☐	
10. Is multi-section learning data used only for its intended purpose and shared with all stakeholders?	☐	☐	☐	

Figure 12: Sustainability Tool—Course (Multi-Section) Level, 4 of 4

Sustainability Tool: Instructor Level				
Use this rating scale when assessing each indicator under the 5 critical factors. Y – yes, done consistently N – No, not on radar NI – needs improvement				
Purpose of this tool:	To provide a systems and an appreciative inquiry approach to examine course alignment of outcomes, content, learning activities, and assessment tasks to ensure that valid assessment results can be produced. Without alignment, learners may not be able to provide evidence of learning outcomes because they are not prepared or not asked to provide appropriate learning evidence.			
Who should use this tool?	Each instructor that teaches a course.			
How do you use this tool?	Use as a guide to examine the five factors—one at a time. Make adjustments that will improve alignment and the flow of learning evidence.			
When do you use this tool?	• As a starting point to evaluate alignment and determine any improvements. • When planning to teach a new course. It will guide decisions about learning activities, assessment tasks, and assignments.			

Outcomes and Professional Standards Alignment	Y	N	NI	Notes
1. Do the learning outcomes for this course align with any of the organization-wide outcomes?	☐	☐	☐	
2. Do the learning outcomes for this course align with any of the outcomes of any program?	☐	☐	☐	
3. Do the learning outcomes for this course align with any professional or certification standards associated with this course?	☐	☐	☐	
Outcomes and Content Alignment	Y	N	NI	Notes
1. Is the content (*concepts*, *skills* and *issues*) in this course relevant to real-life roles?	☐	☐	☐	
2. Do the concepts learned in this course contribute to course, program, and/or organization-wide learning outcomes?	☐	☐	☐	
3. Do the *issues* learners must resolve in this course contribute to course, program, and/or organization-wide learning outcomes?	☐	☐	☐	
4. Do the *skills* developed in this course contribute to course, program, and/or organization-wide learning outcomes?	☐	☐	☐	

Figure 13: Sustainability Tool—Instructor Level, 1 of 2

Sustainability Tool: Instructor Level				
Use this rating scale when assessing each indicator under the 5 critical factors. Y – yes, done consistently N – No, not on radar NI – needs improvement				
Outcome, Learning Activities, and Assignments Alignment	**Y**	**N**	**NI**	**Notes**
1. Do the learning activities align with course, program, and/or organization-wide learning outcomes?	☐	☐	☐	
2. Do the assignments align with course, program, and/or organization-wide learning outcomes?	☐	☐	☐	
3. Are the learning activities relevant to the real-life roles?	☐	☐	☐	
4. Are the assignments relevant to the real-life roles?	☐	☐	☐	
Outcomes and Assessment Tasks and Test Alignment	**Y**	**N**	**NI**	**Notes**
1. Do the assessment tasks and tests used in this course provide evidence of the course learning outcomes?	☐	☐	☐	
2. Do the assessment tasks and tests used in this course provide evidence of the program and/or organization learning outcomes?	☐	☐	☐	
Learning Outcome Evidence Cycling	**Y**	**N**	**NI**	**Notes**
1. Are learning results tracked and made available to other instructors who have an invested interest in how well learners have done in this course?	☐	☐	☐	
2. Is learning evidence used to make adjustments in the delivery, next time around?	☐	☐	☐	
3. Is learning evidence used to update course documents that reflect the changes that need to be made by all instructors?	☐	☐	☐	

Figure 13: Sustainability Tool—Instructor Level, 2 of 2

PART THREE
Creating and Sustaining an Outcomes and Assessment System through Effective Leadership

Changing a whole system requires sustained leadership.

Creating and Sustaining an Outcomes and Assessment System through Effective Leadership

The Challenge of Leading Deep and Complex Change

There was a simpler time in higher education; there was a simpler time in life. But rather than wish for the return to what may have been simpler times, we need to find ways to make things as simple as possible within the context of an increasingly complex world.

There was also a time when building curriculum was a matter of dividing the world of knowledge into disciplines, dividing disciplines into themes, dividing themes into courses, dividing courses into topics and dividing topics into lectures that could be delivered in 50-minute blocks. The curriculum consisted of one-sentence descriptions of thousands of courses in an impressive 3-inch thick catalog; courses generated credits and credits culminated in degrees.

Today, good or bad, most of these things are still true except that the catalog is now on-line, and there is a whole new *overlay*.

Since change of this nature takes root within the culture of the old, the outcomes and assessment initiative of the past twenty years has been laid on top of old paradigms and structures. The *overlay* adds complexity by advocating for collaboration with the real world, identifying learning outcomes, aligning content with outcomes, using work quality assessment strategies, and using learning evidence to improve the learner's experience. It's a dynamic learner-center model in a static content-based framework.

To further complicate matters, an *outcomes and assessment system* brings with it a new language, a different concept of teaching commonly referred to as active learning, and a positive regard for interdisciplinary learning which is essential for the achievement of most real-life outcomes.

It's no wonder it's complex. But even when we get to the point where the outcome-based notion is no longer an overlay, outcome-based curriculum development work will still be more complex than a curriculum that merely organizes subject content into discrete blocks of knowledge. Here is why.

What makes an outcome-based system complex are the same things that make it a dynamic system: *1) interdependence, 2) emergence, and 3) self-adjustment.*

Interdependence

In contrast to the strong sense of autonomy that higher education instructors have experienced in the past, an outcome-based system requires a sense of interdependence. When curricular planning begins outside the classroom with this question: *What do learners need to do "out there" as a result of their preparation "in here,"* relationships begin to matter. It is a question that can't be answered in the isolation of the academy. It is answered by working with potential employers, community leaders, gatekeepers to the professions, instructors in other disciplines, and learners themselves. In an outcome-based curriculum, a curriculum designer does not alone build the curriculum, nor does an instructor. It requires a collaborative and collective effort on the part of many.

Emergence

Continual adaptation and change, which is a natural part of every living system on the earth, is also reflected in an outcome-based curriculum. And it is a process that has little resemblance to the 2-year process used in many colleges to change a single course. Where a 3-inch thick college catalog appears fixed and static, an outcome-based system never stands still and can appear quite chaotic.

An artist friend of ours tells of traveling the Oregon coast on many occasions and attempting to paint the surf without much success. Her comment was, "It just wouldn't hold still!" Same here—the revision of one organization-wide outcome can initiate change in a program outcome which, in turn, may change a course outcome, a lecture, a power-point presentation, and even an assessment tool or test. Our expectation for an outcomes and assessment system should be: *It doesn't hold still.*

Self-adjustment

It is sad to have to say that higher education, in general, has never had a strong reputation for using its own research capacity to renew itself. Perhaps it's the same story as the cobbler's children who have no shoes, but learning outcomes and assessment have the potential to change that. Through the development of assessment tasks that are relevant to real-life roles, the development of effective work quality assessment tools, and the tracking of learning evidence, we can have the data we need to continuously improve what we do. We just have to look around us to see that it's how living systems are sustained.

As if increased complexity weren't enough, creating and sustaining an outcome-based curriculum requires what we might call *deep change*. While many colleges begin with superficial change, *deep change* requires more than adding outcome statements to content-driven syllabi and using new curriculum templates. This *deep change* we speak of includes:

- committing to greater accountability,
- perforating disciplinary boundaries,
- leaving behind our *old schooling* traditions,
- sharing control,
- building relationships inside and outside the college, and
- raising outcome expectations.

These are the kinds of changes that require *deep* and *complex changes* across the college, and it requires sustained, effective leadership.

Leadership at Three Different Levels

While leadership can be defined in many different ways, in establishing and sustaining an outcomes and assessment system in higher education, the definition that says it best might be: *having the courage to go first and put oneself at risk to open a path for others to follow.* Going first and opening the path happens at four different levels of the curriculum: program level, organization level, course level (multi-section) and instructor level.

We talked earlier about programs being *ground-zero* for building an outcome-based curriculum. So it follows that competent and sustained leadership at the program level is most often the flame that ignites the work and does the most to sustain the work over time.

We have observed on campus after campus that the early embers that ignite outcomes thinking are found first at the program level, and most often in technical, science and health-related disciplines like nursing. It is there that we so often find leaders who *go first and lead the way* for the whole campus. We assume this is because of the strong relationships these programs have with agencies and businesses outside the college, in real-world contexts. They understand accountability and coordination.

For example, Michele Decker, co-author of The CONTENT Primer, *leads a nursing program at Central Oregon Community College, but her influence on outcomes and assessment planning extends far beyond the nursing program. While the college has strong campus-wide leaders, she is often the go-to person for other program coordinators on outcomes and assessment. Leading means going first; going first means leading.*

Meanwhile, in the past five years, most colleges have recognized the need to have someone at the organization level *assist* in the creation of a unified system for outcomes and assessment. (Notice our choice of the word *assist* which acknowledges that building an outcomes and assessment system is a collaborative process.)

Colleges across the nation have found that selecting a person to coordinate outcomes and assessment across the college is now essential, but it is also essential to select the right person. In many of the early appointments, whoever was available became the outcomes and assessment coordinator without professional preparation for the work. Most of the time, these appointments didn't accomplish much and didn't last long.

As more people gain practical experience and appropriate academic preparation in outcomes and assessment systems, college-wide leadership is improving. In many situations, colleges are growing their own leaders.

For example, Lori Sours, a co-author on The OUTCOME Primer, *became the lead outcomes and assessment strate-gist at her college after going first as an instructor and a department chair while working closely with knowledgeable consultants. In addition, her research background from her doctoral program prepared her well for gathering and analyzing learning data.*

It's this kind of experience and academic preparation that colleges can now expect from the person who leads the way at the organization level.

The third level of leadership is at the course level, when multiple sections of the same course are offered and staffed by adjunct instructors. It is especially important that the lead faculty member *go first and lead the way* in implementing an outcomes and assessment structure that is consistent across all sections of the course.

Becoming the Leaders We Want to Be

In PART TWO of this Primer, we focused on four Sustainability Tools (one at each level of the organization) that can be used to gauge the major factors that affect the sustainability of any outcomes and assessment system. One of the four major factors in each of the tools is leadership. Under leadership, we identified the factors that might indicate effective leadership.

We have provided here a set of questions, shown in Figure 14 on the following page, to self-assess the roles you can play as *leader* in the learning outcomes and assessment initiative. As you look at these questions, take the time to reflect on your own capacity to *lead* in this work. Each question follows with an accompanying explanation detailing the specific leadership qualities. It is our hope that each question speaks to you personally.

Am I a committed champion of learning outcomes and assessment?

In order to lead, we must be committed to the vision we have of a curriculum driven by learning outcomes and self-adjusting through the assessment of how well learners are able to demonstrate the intended learning outcomes. It is very hard work, and without this commitment, it is impossible work.

To what extent am I good at communicating the vision of an outcomes and assessment system with instructors and stakeholders so there is shared meaning?

There are many different interpretations of words associated with outcomes and assessment planning. It is up to us to see that our language is consistent and that the meaning of each word is shared. This begins with adopting a glossary of outcomes and assessment terms for the organization and doesn't stop until it is the language used by everyone.

Do I seek to engage others from both inside and outside the college to create, refine and review intended learning outcomes, their assessment, and related processes?

It is impossible to do this work alone. The extent to which we are able to get the larger community engaged will determine the sustainability of the system, with or without our contribution.

Do I see my leadership work as one link in a lasting, sustainable system that includes planning for succession?

Effective leaders look beyond their own tenure by preparing others to do what they are doing.

Outcomes and assessment systems are abandoned every day through failure to plan for succession in leadership.

Do I lead in celebrating the efforts of instructors and staff to gather, track and use learning evidence to better serve learners?

The work for everyone is made easier when achievements are recognized by the leaders. It costs nothing, but returns much.

Do I work to foster the trust of my colleagues by being consistent, reliable, respectful, and accountable for an effective outcomes and assessment system?

Trust is so very important in this work that we devote PART SEVEN in this Primer to this question alone.

The leader of the past knew well how to tell. The leader of the future will know how to ask.

—Peter Drucker

Figure 14: How well do I lead?

Leadership Requires Planning for Transition and Succession

Like every dog, leaders have a tendency to want their own fire hydrant.
—Barbara Bessey

There is always risk in leadership transition; it's the opportunity for gain and the threat of loss. Previous gains can be lost and previous losses can be regained; we have seen it both ways in the leadership for outcomes and assessment efforts at all levels of the organization. One of the greatest losses is the loss of continuity when new leaders disregard what already exists in favor of *their new way*.

While we have described an academic program as *ground-zero* for curricular planning, leaders who have the greatest influence over sustainability are found *at the top* in central administration—the persons who provide the resources and appoint the other leaders: presidents, provosts, instructional deans, academic deans, assessment officers, institutional research directors, curriculum directors, curriculum coordinators, and faculty development coordinators.

Transition at the top

If the curriculum belongs to everyone, it might seem that hiring a new president or provost would have little effect on the college curriculum. It is a risky assumption. Here are two different scenarios about transition in leadership. A college we first worked with more than ten years ago had established one of the most effective outcomes and assessment systems in the nation.

Scenario: The Senior Vice President of Academic Affairs, the Dean of Arts and Science, and the Assessment Coordinator were the champions; all three were deeply trusted by faculty across the entire campus. On numerous occasions, the college received national recognition for the model they put in place.

Little did any one expect the impact on this model assessment program when the Board of Trustees decided to not renew contracts for anyone at the senior leadership level.

Not only had the college lost its top champion for learning assessment, under the new President and Vice President for Academic Affairs, the assessment coordinator position was eliminated. In the following six years, the Vice President position turned over two more times while no one maintained what had been a model of an outcomes and assessment system.

For a short time, the system survived; portfolios of work continued to be submitted by learners, learning results continued to be tracked by instructors, and data continued to be used for purposes of program improvement through the dedicated efforts of instructors. But little attention was given to maintaining any college-wide system for learning outcomes and assessment.

Time went by rapidly and soon the college faced another accreditation visit. When it was over, the report from the accreditation committee began with the words: **What happened to such a stellar system?** *After another delay of several years, the college responded by appointing a new outcomes and assessment coordinator who now seeks to restore and rebuild the work.*

We asked the long-time Senior Vice-President of Academic Affairs, Dr. Judith Maxson (now retired from Hocking College), to share with us what she believes are the keys to sustainability of an outcomes and assessment system. Here is what she told us:

1. Assure that academic programs are current with regular review of intended learning outcomes identifying what graduates need to be able to DO "out there" (rest of life) that we are responsible for "in here" (college/program/course).

2. Deliver frequent, consistent messages about the importance of outcome-based education, curriculum mapping, and assessment of student academic achievement.

3. Emphasize that outcome-based education, curriculum mapping, and assessment of student academic achievement must be faculty-driven processes.

4. Identify and support a leader for outcome-based education, curriculum mapping and assessment.

5. Provide extensive professional development and support related to outcome-based education, curriculum mapping, and assessment so that all faculty and academic administrators are knowledgeable about and implement these processes.

6. Set aside time for analysis of assessment data and decisions regarding outcomes, curriculum, and instruction to provide for continuous improvement.

7. Assure continuity in academic and institutional expectations for and support of outcome-based education, curriculum mapping, and assessment of student academic achievement.

Scenario: At a very large university on the East Coast, transition in top leadership had the opposite effect. The college hired a new vice provost who had worked at a West Coast university with an outcome-based curriculum and was committed to the work. By using the work that had already been done, she was able to create and sustain an outcomes and assessment initiative that benefits as many as 60,000 learners around the world. Transition in top leadership brought new opportunities to this university.

It is important in thinking about transitions in leadership that we not confuse *sustainability* with *stability*. Neither of the above scenarios brought stability; both brought change and a degree of instability. As strange as it may sound, it is common to find that the road to sustainability is through instability and change. All living systems function in an unstable, dynamic state ready for change. *In curriculum planning, stability is not the state we seek; sustainability through self-adjustment is what we seek.*

Transition at the program and course levels

Mid-level leadership for outcomes and assessment usually resides with the position of a program director, program coordinator, department head, or a lead instructor when there are multiple sections of a single course.

Because there are usually several faculty who are involved in on-going curriculum planning at the program level, it is likely that transition in leadership is less problematic than at the organization level. The more a program instructor functions in bringing together a core

of instructors working as a team, the greater chance that all program functions will be sustained through personnel transitions. It's when faculty function autonomously under the premise of academic freedom that the whole program suffers, and especially, the gathering, tracking, and use of learning evidence. An added challenge is including adjunct instructors as part of the team.

Here is an example of good succession planning at the program level.

Lynn Null, co-author of The ASSESSMENT Primer, left her leadership position in a Childhood Development Program at Western Oklahoma College for a position as director of a county extension service in the same state. Long before she had ever thought about making a career change, she and her faculty had developed one of the first nationally-accredited on-line programs for child development workers in the country. The key here was that she had fully engaged all the instructors during the two years of development work.

While every instructor's capacity for leading the work increased, one of the instructors stood out. While there was no formal succession plan, an informal plan emerged as a direct result of Lynn's collaborative leadership style. Whether formal or informal, succession planning is essential to program sustainability.

Creating and Sustaining an Outcomes and Assessment System through Instructor Involvement

There is nothing more foundational to outcomes thinking than to carry a mental image of paddlers on a white-water journey through unfamiliar rapids with a guide at the back.

Creating and Sustaining an Outcomes and Assessment System through Instructor Involvement

Instructor as Engaged Learner

In the Preface to this Primer, we spoke about those traits that have distinguished our work with learning outcomes and assessment initiatives over the years; one is a deep commitment to active learning, not only for developing learners, but also for instructor development. We have highlighted this commitment to active learning by creating the image of a paddle raft on a whitewater river where the paddlers are engaged in the serious work of getting themselves and the guide down the river. Being in a paddle raft is very different from being in an oar raft where the guide has two oars and *the river rats* (the participants) are disengaged from paddling, and simply tasked with holding on tight and going along for the ride.

This contrast between the *oar raft* and the *paddle raft* summarizes not only two very different ways instructors teach in higher education, but how leaders teach instructors in implementing new systems. Leaders can take the *oars* and ask the instructors to ride along, or they can choose to give every instructor a *paddle* and *guide* them to the intended outcome (*take-out*). The idea here is leader as *guide*—providing the instructors with the skills and resources they need to engage in making the system work.

The process of getting instructors engaged is best described In *The GUIDING Primer: Guiding Toward Learning Outcomes*, where we tell the story of a staff in-service day on a wild whitewater river in the high desert of Oregon. Told in the voice of Jackie, the coordinator of a joint college program on alternative energy technology, the story is based on our work through the Whitewater Institute for Leadership Training, *www.white-waterinstitute.org*.

If we could, we would take every outcomes and assessment coordinator with us to the river to see what engaged learning really looks like. But, for you, the reader, we have to settle here for telling part of the story.

Our purpose for telling a portion of the story here is to help you envision the importance of involving your college's instructors as engaged learners in building an effective outcomes and assessment system. As you read this story, look for the strategies, techniques and practices Twyla, an experienced river guide, uses to get her paddlers engaged. These are the same strategies, techniques, and practices that will engage instructors in developing a sustainable outcomes and assessment system across the organization.

The Story

Set-up: This story is set on a whitewater river at the base of the Cascade Mountains in Eastern Oregon. It is told by Jackie Peterson, coordinator of a college program, who takes her instructional staff of seven educators on a whitewater journey as part of a staff-in-service opportunity. She contracts with a seasonal whitewater guide, Twyla,

who also has years of experience as an innovative classroom teacher.

Twyla, exemplary guide

As you read through this story, reflect on these two important questions:

1) What does Twyla, the river guide, do to involve her paddlers so that they are engaged in the journey at all times?

2) What can we learn from the story that suggests what we need to do to get instructors fully

engaged in curriculum design and assessment work? Following each chapter of the story, we summarize some of these ideas.

The Boathouse: *The sun was fully up as we drove across the wheat fields on our early morning approach to Maupin, Oregon, year-round population of 612 (which might be pushing it a bit). We quickly lost the sun as we descended 900 feet into the Deschutes River canyon, proceeded down Main Street (all three blocks) and crossed the river on the old stone bridge.*

Twyla, our river guide for the day, worked out of Maupin's only skyscraper, a 120-year-old wooden elevator no longer used for grain storage—the risk of fire in the old timbers was far too great. The bottom floor now served as a boathouse for several different rafting companies, which made up the city's largest industry.

As we pulled into the parking area, it was already an active scene around the boathouse—colorful kayaks on car roofs, aluminum dory boats on trailers, stacks of rainbow colored rafts just inside the big doors and a host of Bureau of Land Management rangers looking for river rats without a license to be on the river.

*As soon as we stepped out of the college van, **Twyla was there in the doorway to meet us.** I had forgotten just how small she looked—couldn't be more than 120 pounds, yet she could out-perform anyone on the river; she had been doing it for so many years that the young guides lovingly called her "grandma."*

I had brought to the river a motley looking group of seven instructors who had been in the van since 4:30 a.m. As we followed Twyla into the boathouse, most of us were in bad need of that second cup of coffee.

We all had critical things to attend to: two adjunct instructors from industry, Greg and Delco, scouted the boathouse quickly, spotted the snack counter and made a dash for the coffee machine; Bernie wasn't far behind; Dr. Olmsted and PJ Plunket went for a donut and soda; Jennifer and I passed on food; Sonny found the restroom.

*Two very young guides, Jason and Topher, whispered to Twyla (our assigned guide), "Glad this is your group." Knowing I overheard it, Twyla turned to me, smiled, and said, **"They are just used to younger folk."***

*Having taken care of the most important things, we all turned our attention to **Twyla** who first **wanted to know if all of us knew why we had come all this way to the river.** In our last staff meeting, when I (Jackie) first explained the unusual nature of this in-service day, the responses had been mixed. I could see, as we stood there together, some were more aware than others. Both Twyla and I knew **the key was to make sure everyone sensed that there was real purpose behind what we were about to do.** I left it to Twyla, knowing she would explain it better than I had in my email to her.*

She started out by saying, "This is not Disneyland (long pause); this is a wild river. Perhaps not terribly different than your or my classrooms (a chuckle).

When we journey together down this river, we will face the challenges not unlike those our learners face.

*Our task in our courses is to achieve the outcomes we want. **The first and most important outcome for us today is for you and me to get down the river safely— with you doing the paddling.***

Yes, guides don't have oars here.

You and I will only have paddles. This means you need to right away develop paddling skills and learn how to read the river. Our lives depend on it."

I looked around at the different expressions.

*One sure thing—**no one was any longer asleep!***

Twyla continued, "But our intentions today go far beyond just getting to the take-out. Like you, next week I go back to the classroom, in my case, an on-line classroom. And when I do, I will guide my learners using the same practices that work for me so well here on the river—every fall term a fresher perspective."

Twyla continued, "When I return to the classroom each fall, I take a couple new practices with me—things I have tried on the river but have not yet perfected.

*I work on them all year. I am hoping the same for you by the time we finish today. **The intent is for you to be able to identify specific guiding practices and set them as your own professional development goals for this next year.** In everything you observe and everything you experience today, watch for what speaks to you...a couple things that deserve some attention and will make you a better guide."*

After signing some insurance forms, we exited the Boathouse to find an old bus, an old man and a trailer with three rafts ready to move out. Only one raft was for us— the other two were for the young guides, Topher and Jason, and their groups of high schoolers. I was glad I was with the crowd I had brought.

As we boarded the bus, I knew we had some very clear intended outcomes for this experience, but I also knew that each of us would take away many other "unintended," but no less significant, lessons from the river. That's how a river works; that's how life works; that's how educational programs should work.

How Twyla Engaged the Paddlers on the River	How Leaders Can Engage Instructors in Outcomes and Assessment Work
"Twyla was there in the doorway to meet us."	Welcome them and make them feel important; work with them, start to finish.
"They are just used to younger folk."	Relax, use a little humor.
"Twyla...wanted to know if all of us knew why we had come all this way to the river."..."the key was to make sure everyone sensed that there was real purpose behind what we were about to do."	Clarify the purpose of every work session, more than once. Identify clear and robust learning outcomes for work sessions.
"The first and most important outcome for us today is for you and me to get down the river safely—with you doing the paddling."	Always state the intended learning outcomes when working with instructors.
"Yes, guides don't have oars here. You and I will have paddles."	Share the control; share the work.
"...no one was any longer asleep!"	Create interesting activities
"The intent is for you to be able to identify specific guiding practices and set them as your own professional development goals for this next year."	Focus on outcomes and discuss the intent of the outcomes identified with instructors.

Figure 15: Summary of Twyla's Actions—The Boathouse

The Bus: *Tired school buses line the streets of little rafting towns like Maupin. Some still run, others don't. Willy's ran.*

To describe Willy's bus was to describe Willy himself. It was hard to separate the two: tall, strong, old, weather-beaten and fiercely dependable.

As we all got to know Willy (and it didn't take long), there was nothing offensive about the "girlie" slogan on his hat, which was in perfect keeping with the tattoo of the South Pacific beauty on his arm. Willy had lived a lot of lives in a lot of places before becoming part of this river experience, which he truly was.

After three grinds and a couple false starts, Willy set out downriver on a narrow river access road which had once been a railroad track.

It was 15 minutes on the washboard before we rolled to a stop at a place called Sandy Beach, where in the far distance we saw that the river fell away into a deeper canyon. It was a sure thing that we wouldn't be putting in here.

*Twyla stood and explained. "I asked Willy to bring us here first; this is the take-out— the very spot we want to get to later this afternoon. **I wanted you to see the destination.** What each of you learn to do in the next few hours is what will get us here—or not." It was part of Twyla's practice as a guide to show us the finish line first while Willy pulled out a large map of the river that showed the whole run, put-in to take-out with the rapids clearly marked.*

*Twyla continued. "On our drive back upriver to the put-in above Maupin, we are going to scout each of the rapids from the road. **We want you to see the big picture and know what to expect."***

Willy turned and headed us back upriver; his eyes were glued to the narrow roadway between the river and the canyon wall, while ours were fixed on the water.

*In no time at all, **Twyla pointed to what would be our greatest challenge—Oak Springs Rapid.** From the bus window, we could see where a boulder the size of two buses split the river into two chutes: the right side, a difficult Class IV rapid; the left, a Class III rapid. Except for the teenagers on the bus, our team sat speechless through the whole trip, but we hadn't experienced anything yet.*

*Jennifer spoke. "I see it all! We are going to get into one of those tubes and paddle through one of those chutes. Is that the idea?" Twyla assured her, "By the time we get there, we'll be ready. **We'll prove ourselves on the smaller ones before we ever get to Oak Springs."***

How Twyla Engaged the Paddlers on the River	How Leaders Can Engage Instructors in Outcomes and Assessment Work
"I wanted you to see the destination."... "We want you to see the big picture and know what to expect."..."Twyla pointed to what would be our greatest challenge—Oak Springs Rapid."	Take time to share the vision—what it will be like when the work has been accomplished; show examples of end products—good outcome statements, assessment tasks, rubrics, scoring guides, to name a few.
"We'll prove ourselves in the smaller ones (rapids) before we ever get to Oak Springs."	Start with smaller tasks that lead to more challenging ones to build proficiency.

Figure 16: Summary of Twyla's Actions—The Bus

Harpham Flats: *By the time we got to Harpham Flats we had not only had a glimpse of each rapid on Willy's map, but we had seen the flat-water between the rapids.*

It would be in flat-water that we would learn what was needed to get successfully through each rapid.

Harpham Flats, the put-in spot, was unlike Sandy Beach. Here the river bank was strewn with boulders and the water seemed to "giggle and laugh as it teased the shore," which was how Jennifer described it when we stepped from the bus.

While everyone I invited had taught in the Alternative Energy Program for at least a year, we hadn't really worked closely together. **As with many instructors, they were never at the same place at the same time, even though they worked with the same learners.** *While being able to work together wasn't one of the intended outcomes for this in-service, it was still a desirable outcome.*

Twyla directed Jason and Topher's youngsters to get the rafts off the trailer and into the water. She directed the rest of us to help each other put on the life jackets. *Both Willy and Twyla then checked every life jacket to make sure each of us had a snug fit in preparation for our ride on a wild river.*

Once Twyla knew each jacket fit properly, she began her put-in talk. She demonstrated the critical safety measures *we could each take through unpredictable situations including strainers (downed trees) and sleepers (boulders just out of* site below the surface). She told everyone, "To your neighbor, your paddle is the most dangerous thing in the raft," and followed-up by checking everyone's t-grip. Put-in—take-out—strainers—sleepers—paddle raft—t-grip. Without even realizing it, we were beginning to use the language of the river.

Twyla then asked each paddler, **"Is there something else I need to do for any of you before we make our final preparations?"** Dr. Olmsted quickly responded, **"Please put me in the part of the raft where I won't get wet."**

Twyla said, **"Emma (like Willy, calling her by her first name), there probably won't be a dry seat anywhere, but I'll place you right by me at the back, if you would like that."** Ever since she met us at the Boathouse, **Twyla had been getting a sense of who we were as individuals in order to address our needs**. But beyond individual needs, she knew that the only way to get everyone down this river was to work like a community.

Taking a handful of rubber wrist bands from her bag, Twyla divided them by color: blue, red, yellow. "Take a blue band and put it on your right wrist if you consider yourself already pretty skilled in getting down this river—you know you can do it. Take a red band if you have some concerns but not any real fears—you feel you can make it with help from the rest of us. Take yellow if you've never done anything like this and it all feels very scary to you right now."

By having us wear the bands in full sight, we quickly became aware of each other's degree of vulnerability; no one hesitated in selecting a band. In our raft, we had three blues, two reds, and three yellows. Twyla told us, **"Mark my word, we will all be blue or red by the time we finish at Sandy Beach."**

Jason and Topher pushed our raft onto the bank and we proceeded to get in, blues in the front, reds in the middle and yellows at the rear. We quickly found we already had a challenge—stepping onto the spongy floor while trying to keep our balance. Some of us looked like toddlers just learning to walk: one step, fall, another step, down again.

I watched thoughtfully as Twyla pushed the raft from the bank, boarded the rear, and sat high on the tube.

*Sonny whispered in my ear, "Until they gave all of us a paddle, I thought Twyla would be oaring us through the rapids. It's OK with me; **I'd rather do the work myself anyway.**"*

The raft began to drift slowly with the river's current and an undercurrent of excitement stirred within each of us. Jennifer yelled, "No turning back now."

How Twyla Engaged the Paddlers on the River	How Leaders Can Engage Instructors in Outcomes and Assessment Work
"As with many instructors, they were never at the same place at the same time, even though they worked with the same learners."	Plan work session activities that require collaboration; it might just be the only opportunity instructors have to talk with each other.
"Twyla directed Jason and Topher's youngsters to get the rafts off the trailer and into the water. She directed the rest of us to help each other put on the life jackets."	Ask instructors to help each other.
"Once Twyla knew each jacket fit properly, she began her put-in talk. ... She demonstrated the critical safety measures." "Is there something else I need to do for any of you before we make our final preparations?"	Curriculum revision will feel like a threat to some instructors; be sure they feel safe rather than threatened.
Dr. Olmsted quickly responded, "Please put me in the part of the raft where I won't get wet." ... Twyla said, "Emma ... there probably won't be a dry seat anywhere, but I'll place you right by me at the back, if you would like that."	Mentor and keep things safe for all.
"Twyla has been getting a sense of who we were as individuals in order to address our needs" ... "Taking a handful of rubber wrist bands from her bag, Twyla divided them by color: blue, red, yellow."	Be creative; find ways they can assess their own skills.
"Mark my word, we will all be blue or red by the time we finish at Sandy Beach."	Believe in them; tell them you believe in them.
"I'd rather do the work myself anyway." (paddler)	Let the instructors take control of their own learning; we provide the support.

Figure 17: Summary of Twyla's Actions—Harpham Flats

Wapanitia Rapid: *The minute we caught the main current, it dropped us into a long stretch of flat water with intermittent riffles. It was just what we needed to begin to get our act together.* **Putting seven paddles in the water was one thing; using them to control the raft's movement at a moment's notice was something quite different.**

Twyla led from the back:

FORWARD PADDLE

LEFT PADDLE

RIGHT PADDLE

BACK PADDLE

DIG

Twyla taught us the baby steps—strokes and commands. **As we were beginning to feel how the raft responded to our paddles (individually and collectively), we were picking up more of the language—command, dig, left dig, right dig, forward, stop, synchronize.**

We also began learning to read the river: tongue, strainer, eddy, confluence, hole, channel switching, and tube-suck. When we all laughed at tube suck, Twyla assured us we would never fully understand it until we were caught in one; then we would know it, and not ever forget it. She was quick to point out that learning to read the river required more than knowing the language; among other things, it meant you had to listen to the river.

At first, only Twyla and I heard the distant sound of Wapanitia Rapid.

Our time on this long stretch of flat water had gone too fast. The current in the main channel had moved us along quickly and we had been solely focused on our paddles. **I wouldn't have described our skills as synchronized, not yet—not by a long shot—when we headed into this first rapid.**

Twyla called it a wake-up rapid, just big enough to give us a taste of rough water and just time enough to develop a bit of confidence in our paddling skills. It was also a test of our ability to synchronize our strokes with Bernie, the lead paddler at the front left.

FORWARD PADDLE

DIG

KEEP DIGGING

KEEP DIGGING

LINE IT UP

LEFT PADDLE

KEEP PADDLING

Faster than any of us expected, the front of the raft dropped into a hole, pitched us high in the air while torrents of water swamped the back. Up front, Bernie and Jennifer emerged from the hole in a froth of whitewater.

While this first rapid was no big thing on this river, it was a big thing to us. It required that each of us go into action while **Twyla watched it all.**

As soon as we passed through Wapanitia, **Twyla guided us into a small eddy along the right bank, where the river quiets and keeps us from the forward mov-**

ing current. *She wanted us to take notice of Wapanitia Rapid from afar as another raft maneuvered through. Seeing another spongy, over-stuffed tube respond to the current was part of learning to read the river hydraulics in a small rapid, and by comparison, to assess how we had done.*

While eddying-out right after Wapanitia, Twyla also provided feedback for each of us based on what she had observed. ***Twyla's feedback was specific.*** *I don't recall everything she told the others, but I remember her words to me. "When I say 'dig,' you have to paddle through the entire rapid. Don't cut it short, Jackie."*

As I recalled from last year, from here onward, it would be this constant cycle of action—feedback, action—feedback, action—feedback that would most characterize Twyla's relationship with all of us. ***Her observations were constant with the sole thought of assessing to assist us in achieving one of the main outcomes****, which is, navigating successfully through the rapids to get down the river safely.*

As we prepared to paddle back into the current, everyone seemed fully committed to the journey. ***We had been prepared well. We could envision where we were headed. We had scouted our challenges and knew what we had to go through before getting there. We were beginning to feel like a community and for this moment, at least, we had our own specific things to work on.***

How Twyla Engaged the Paddlers on the River	How Leaders Can Engage Instructors in Outcomes and Assessment Work
"Putting nine paddles in the water was one thing; using them to control the raft's movement at a moment's notice was something quite different. *"Twyla led from the back."*	Let the instructors take control of their own learning; allow them to learn from their own mistakes; praise their successes. Mentor always.
"As we were beginning to feel how the raft responded to our paddles (individually and collectively), we were picking up more of the language—command, dig, left dig, right dig, forward, stop, synchronize."	Define the terminology with examples (e.g., outcome statements, mapping, guiding, prototyping, etc.).
"I wouldn't have described our skills as synchronized, not yet—not by a long shot—when we headed into this first rapid.... Twyla called it a wake-up rapid, just big enough to give us a taste of rough water."	Provide on-going assessments used to assist in developing their skills; there should be no grading or testing.
"Twyla watched it all."	Constantly observe and mentor.
"Twyla guided us into a small eddy along the right bank, where the river quiets and keeps us from the forward moving current. Twyla's feedback was specific."	Take time for reflection and give specific, timely feedback to improve the work and keep them progressing.
"Her observations were constant with the sole thought of assessing to assist us in achieving one of the main outcomes."	Focus and remind them of the intended learning outcomes for each work session.
"We had been prepared well. We could envision where we were headed. We had scouted our challenges and knew what we had to go through before getting there. We were beginning to feel like a community and for this moment, at least, we had our own specific things to work on."	Prepare them well; envision next steps; be honest about the challenges; build community; be sure everyone knows what work they need to do.

Figure 18: Summary of Twyla's Actions—Wapanitia Rapid

Boxcar Rapid: *As we moved through flat water, with Boxcar still a fair distance ahead, we quickly learned that even flat water isn't always flat and it also has its challenges.*

For one thing, flat water is slow and boring, which **seemed to be just what we needed for repetitive practice.**

Not very far into the calm, flat stretch, we passed directly over what Twyla called a sleeper—a large rock so close to the surface we couldn't see it until we felt it.

We experienced what river rats call a tube suck. It's enough just to say we were lucky we got out of it with everyone still in the raft, while Twyla didn't miss a beat in making it a teachable moment.

"What would we have done had we high-centered back there? That was a real possibility, you know. The simple paddling skills we needed for Wapanitia wouldn't have been enough." **So, she put us through a new series of paddling drills by simulating another sleeper.**

We heard Boxcar before we could see it and anxiously squirmed into our paddling positions. Twyla had shown Bernie and Jennifer again how to anchor their feet tightly under the thwarts. We followed their lead. Over the increasing background noise, Twyla gave her first commands.

PADDLE FORWARD

LEFT SIDE FORWARD

RELAX

FORWARD THREE STROKES

REST

STOP

I felt a strong bounce and my body sank deeper into the raft. **Twyla used her paddle to move us to the left of the pillow.** *Then it all happened so fast. We brushed the side of a boulder on the left and caught sight of a strainer to the right. Twyla called out:*

BACK PADDLE

STOP.

In a matter of seconds, we moved past the fallen tree into shallow, choppy water.

DIG, DIG, DIG!

KEEP DIGGING!

We hit the second drop, then the third. We quickly regained speed, dipping and turning with the current, when a standing wave broadsided Delco and PJ.

Twyla's voice was excited and serious. The whole raft was swamped. Delco lost his balance and fell back into Dr. Olmsted.

When the raft shot upward, then leveled out, it seemed we were safely through the rapid.

But no! Delco was out of the raft and it had happened so quickly!

Twyla called to Sonny to grab Delco.

Holding his paddle backwards and reaching far out over the side of the raft, Delco was clearly over-extended when PJ jumped up and took a tight hold on Sonny's life jacket. In no more than 10 seconds, Delco was back in the raft. No need for the throw-bag.

This was evidence that Twyla and the river had guided us well. **We raised our paddles in a salute to our success.**

How Twyla Engaged the Paddlers on the River	How Leaders Can Engage Instructors in Outcomes and Assessment Work
"... seemed to be just what we needed for repetitive practice."	Give time for practice-building skills requires practice.
"We experienced what river rats call a tube suck. It's enough just to say we were lucky we got out of it with everyone still in the raft, while Twyla didn't miss a beat in making it a teachable moment."	Let them take risks; then provide ways for improvement.
"So, she put us through a new series of paddling drills by simulating another sleeper."	Use simulation when you can't do the real thing.
"Twyla used her paddle to move us to the left of the pillow."	Know when to step in and help.
"We raised our paddles in a salute to our success."	Celebrate every success together.

Figure 19: Summary of Twyla's Actions—Boxcar Rapid

Our purpose in telling part of this unusual in-service story was to focus our attention on instructors as learners and what got them fully engaged. The most obvious thing Twyla did, of course, was to put them on a real river and place paddles in their hands. She didn't talk about the river or give a power-point presentation with pictures of the river—she engaged them in the real thing, little by little. Might this suggest that the way to get instructors engaged in all instances is to hand them the tools (outcome guides, scoring guides, assessment tools) and guide from the back as they work through the challenges in curriculum design and assessment planning?

Involving Instructors in the Outcomes and Assessment Effort

There are five essential tasks in building and sustaining an outcomes and assessment system at the program, course and organization levels in which teams of instructors should be involved. These include: 1) envisioning learning outcome statements, 2) aligning essential content with intended outcomes, 3) developing assessment criteria and tools, 4) mapping the learner's journey through a program or a course, and 5) using learning evidence to improve one's own practices.

Like planning for and engaging paddlers together on a whitewater river, planning and engaging instructors together in challenging *work sessions* is the way to assure their involvement in building a sustainable outcomes and assessment system. Note that we did not call them workshops; too often workshops become presentations that discourage real engagement. This distinction is important; in a *work session*, real work is accomplished and instructors do the *paddling*. The facilitator guides from the back toward a very specific intended outcome—often times, a product.

Several of the Primers in this series contain a *Facilitator Guide* with step-by-step directions for facilitating outcomes and assessment *work sessions* with administrators, instructors and even external advisory groups. What follows are the titles and sources of each Facilitator Guide in this series followed by one full example of how they engage instructors.

Facilitator Guides in *The Outcome Primers Series 2.0* (TOPS)

Developing Significant Outcomes:
Involving instructional staff and stakeholders in the creation of learning outcomes. (Source: *The OUTCOMES Primer: Envisioning Learning Outcomes*, by Stiehl and Sours).

Determining Essential Content:
Involving instructional staff in aligning essential content with learning outcomes. (Source: *The CONTENT Primer: Aligning Essential Content with Learning Outcomes*, by Stiehl and Decker).

Prototyping Assessment Criteria at the Course or Workshop Level:
Involving instructional staff in developing assessment criteria at the course or workshop level. (Source: *The ASSESSMENT Primer: Assessing and Tracking Evidence of Learning Outcomes*, by Stiehl and Null).

Prototyping Assessment Criteria at the Program Level:
Involving instructional staff in developing assessment criteria at the program level. (Source: *The ASSESSMENT Primer: Assessing and Tracking Evidence of Learning Outcomes*, by Stiehl and Null).

Mapping Programs:
Involving program instructors in mapping their program. (Source: *The MAPPING Primer: Mapping the Way to Learning Outcomes*, by Stiehl and Telban).

None of these Facilitator Guides is designed to stand entirely alone, but should be used in conjunction with readings from the appropriate Primer. The more participants understand before attending a work session, the more you will be able to accomplish with them in the limited time you have.

In addition to involving instructors in these critical activities, they should also:

- understand their role and any related committee/department roles and responsibilities for outcomes and assessment,
- be included in assessing learners' work (i.e. learning artifacts),
- be made aware of learner performance on end-of-course/program assessments and involved in the discussion of potential changes based on learning data,
- be involved in developing and improving assessment systems, policy and culture,

- foster trust by being consistent, reliable, respectful and accountable for learning outcome and assessment, and
- take advantage of professional development opportunities to build learning outcomes and assessment knowledge and skills.

Here is a story that describes both when and how to involve instructors in work sessions to design outcome-based curriculum from the beginning.

One of our outcome strategists (Lori) assumed responsibility for guiding instructors in the development of four brand new allied health programs and within a period of 10 months. Not a small task! The college received the grant at the end of September, and by November, Lori was conducting work sessions with instructors and advisory groups—external experts from the field.

In early January, Lori facilitated program mapping work sessions that identified existing courses that aligned with the newly created program outcomes and identified what new courses would be needed. To keep the work moving in follow-up work sessions, the participants determined the type of assessment tasks that would provide the best evidence of meeting the program outcomes. Working on assessment strategies as part of the mapping process not only saved time later, it informed which courses would generate assessment data used to improve the program.

By mid-January, the new courses were created by instructors with external experts during more facilitated work sessions. In a total of three months, four programs were designed and submitted to the college and approved by early February in time to meet the state deadline.

Working from the program outcomes and assessment plans, instructors developed the new courses, the assessment tools to be used at the program level, and course handouts. In Fall of 2016, a total of nearly 60 learners entered the four programs.

Each of the facilitated work sessions that Lori conducted was the key to developing outcome-based programs from the beginning in such a short amount of time. The Facilitator's Guides in the companion Primers help you do the same.

As an example of how carefully our facilitator's guides are focused on assisting instructors in getting the work done, we include in Appendix C an example from *The Outcome Primer: Envisioning Learning Outcomes.*

PART FIVE

Creating and Sustaining an Outcomes and Assessment System through Professional Development

The best part of learning is sharing what you know.

—Vaughn K. Lauer

Introduction: Rising to the Challenge of Professional Development

In-house professional development opportunities in teaching and learning for college instructors and staff vary greatly within the field of higher education. Some institutions make the assumption that none is necessary—all instructors know how to build a curriculum and teach it. So, some colleges focus their professional development efforts exclusively on new and adjunct instructors while others offer a smorgasbord of options for anyone who takes an interest.

Rising to the challenge of professional development in outcomes and assessment efforts means something quite different than any of the above. *It means designing and implementing outcome-based in-service experiences for all staff in the same manner that we design outcome-based learning experiences for our learners.* Sorry to say it might surprise some of us, but instructors and administrators, too, are learners.

In order to fully implement and sustain a curriculum that is driven by external outcomes, and to sustain it through the use of learning evidence across all college programs, professional development opportunities are *essential for everyone* and must be sustained over time. That is the challenge to which we must rise.

Terminology: The Place to Begin

One of the first things we ask a college with whom we are consulting is, "Have you adopted a set of terms you are using across the college to discuss outcomes and assessment?" The typical answer is, "We borrowed ours from another college," or "We've been talking about that; do you have one?" We ask this question early because we know there are real differences in how learning outcomes and assessment are perceived, described, and defined within a single organization.

Example: I (Kathy) recall clearly one specific conversation I had with a group of high-level college administrators when the conversation turned to assessment. As I listened to each of them, I quickly realized they were not talking about the same thing—but they thought they were. Some were talking about course assessment (what instructors do at the end of a course), others were talking about general education outcomes (across the curriculum), while still others were talking about program review. It all seemed so confusing because outcomes and assessment meant different things to each of them and they couldn't see the difference. They didn't see outcomes and assessment at different levels of the organization.

The lesson: Select, define, and use a set of appropriate terms across the entire organization. It is the very foundation of all the planning you will do. Each Primer contains a glossary of terms used in that Primer.

A Professional Development Plan

Overview

It has been our intent in creating *The OUTCOME Primers Series 2.0* (*TOPS*) to provide organizations with the knowledge-base and strategies for creating effective professional development experiences for instructors in outcomes and assessment. In a sense, all six Primers culminate in this section of this Primer.

In fact, it was with in-service professional development in mind that we chose to publish six separate Primers, each with a focus on one particular part of the outcomes and assessment system. While one five-pound Primer would have appeared impressive as a graduate level textbook, it would not have served the thousands of instructors who work with learners in live and virtual classrooms every day. By publishing in small increments, we are able to make the Primers available at a reduced price in sufficient numbers for in-service sessions.

What follows is a structure for designing a complete professional development program in outcomes and assessment based on this series. It includes three major parts:

1. Core *Work Sessions (8)* for all leaders and instructors.

2. *Facilitator Trainings (3)* for in-house outcome and assessment leaders.

3. *Focused Conversations* on the complexities of sustaining the outcomes and assessment system across the organization.

The eight *Core Work* Sessions (2–3 hours) are where staff not only learn more about new outcomes and assessment processes, but work collaboratively to re-design courses *and programs* under the guidance of skilled facilitators. The work is focused and moves quickly, with a typical work session lasting two hours. Work Sessions are not single, isolated events, but regularly-scheduled opportunities for teams to work together on curricular changes over time.

Facilitator Trainings are about preparing a group of in-house facilitators to guide the work sessions on a re-occurring schedule. Facilitators learn to engage groups in well-defined tasks, keep groups focused on the task, keep the energy flowing, conserve time, answer questions, and provide feedback on a group's work. In addition, the facilitators develop the skills necessary to work across all disciplines and at all three levels of the organization. In addition to facilitation skills, they must be fully competent in developing learning outcomes, mapping programs, and creating assessment tools in order to lead others.

Focused Conversations (1-2 hours) concentrate on issues that surface around sustaining an effective outcomes and assessment system across the college. Conversations are sustained by administrators and faculty who recognize issues and are willing to engage in conversation with others. The role of a facilitator is simply to announce the issue, time, and place making it an important part of the professional development agenda. Even when a conversation involves no more than 2–3 persons, it can have meaningful results for both staff and learners. It might take a while to get it started, but it keeps the work moving forward.

Core Work Sessions

Below you will find brief descriptions for the eight *core work sessions* on outcomes and learning assessment. They are listed by name and number and make reference to the specific Primer that contains the knowledge-base for that session. (*You can purchase Primers at a* **discount** *for any one of these work sessions by going to our website* www.outcomeprimers.com.)

Eight (8) Core Work Sessions for All Leaders and Instructors

1. Envisioning and Writing Learning Outcome Statements

2. Aligning Essential Content with Learning Outcomes

3. Assessment: Implementing Work Quality Assessment Strategies

4. Assessment: Creating Work Quality Assessment Tools (Checklists, Scoring Guides, and Rubrics)

5. Mapping the Learner's Journey

6. Mapping Follow-up: Reviewing Second Generation Maps

7. Mapping Follow-up: Third Generation Maps

8. Eight Essential Guiding Practices for Instructors

Work Session Outcome Guides (WOGs)

For each of the core work sessions listed, we include on the next several pages a Work Session Outcome Guide (WOG). A WOG is a one-page template that lays out five critical parts of a curricular plan:

- the *intended learning outcome* for the work session,

- how the learning will be *assessed*,

- what *skills* the participants need to master,

- what *concepts* the participants will need to understand, and

- what issues they will need to be able to resolve to achieve the intended outcome(s).

The power of the WOG is that it describes, on just one page, all the essential things a facilitator needs to have in order to plan learning activities for the session. At the bottom of each WOG is a reference (i.e. resource) to the specific Primer that contains an expanded knowledge-base for the work, and in some cases, step-by step activities for the work. Following each WOG is an example of a product developed from that work session or the assessment tool used to guide and assess the work product produced.

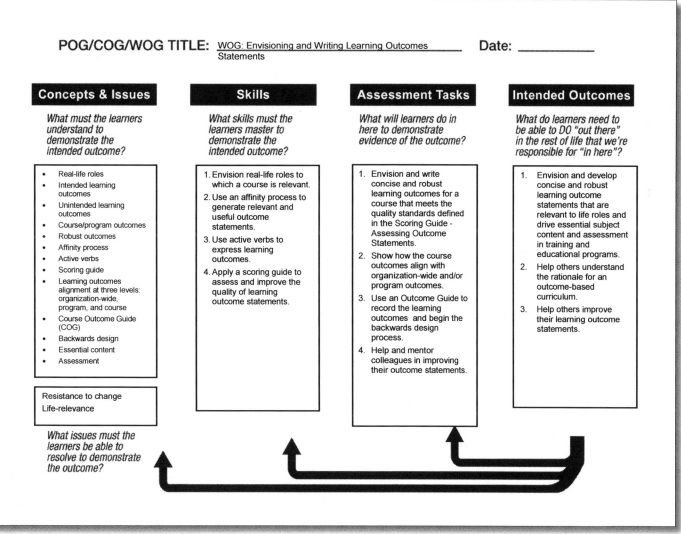

POG/COG/WOG TITLE: WOG: Envisioning and Writing Learning Outcomes Statements   **Date:** _____

Concepts & Issues

What must the learners understand to demonstrate the intended outcome?

- Real-life roles
- Intended learning outcomes
- Unintended learning outcomes
- Course/program outcomes
- Robust outcomes
- Affinity process
- Active verbs
- Scoring guide
- Learning outcomes alignment at three levels: organization-wide, program, and course
- Course Outcome Guide (COG)
- Backwards design
- Essential content
- Assessment

Resistance to change
Life-relevance

What issues must the learners be able to resolve to demonstrate the outcome?

Skills

What skills must the learners master to demonstrate the intended outcome?

1. Envision real-life roles to which a course is relevant.
2. Use an affinity process to generate relevant and useful outcome statements.
3. Use active verbs to express learning outcomes.
4. Apply a scoring guide to assess and improve the quality of learning outcome statements.

Assessment Tasks

What will learners do in here to demonstrate evidence of the outcome?

1. Envision and write concise and robust learning outcomes for a course that meets the quality standards defined in the Scoring Guide - Assessing Outcome Statements.
2. Show how the course outcomes align with organization-wide and/or program outcomes.
3. Use an Outcome Guide to record the learning outcomes and begin the backwards design process.
4. Help and mentor colleagues in improving their outcome statements.

Intended Outcomes

What do learners need to be able to DO "out there" in the rest of life that we're responsible for "in here"?

1. Envision and develop concise and robust learning outcome statements that are relevant to life roles and drive essential subject content and assessment in training and educational programs.
2. Help others understand the rationale for an outcome-based curriculum.
3. Help others improve their learning outcome statements.

Note: Outcomes can be written at three levels: organization, program and course.

Figure 20: WOG: Envisioning and Writing Learning Outcomes Statements
Resource: *The OUTCOME Primer: Envisioning Learning Outcomes*

Samples of Robust Learning Outcome Statements
What should learners be able to DO "out there" that we're responsible for "in here"?

Academic Setting	Workplace Setting
Theme (college-wide): Critical Thinking and Information Resources Think and act with intellectual integrity; access, critically evaluate, and synthesize information from scholarly resources to make and express critical judgments about historical and contemporary issues that affect their lives (social, political, scientific, and personal).	**Leading Change** Champion new ideas, break down barriers and bring about strategic change, in and out of the organization, to meet organizational goals.
Theme (college-wide): Quantitative Reasoning Recognize and interpret the meaning of quantitative symbols and apply quantitative tools and processes to solve problems and make decisions in context.	**Managing Complexity** Analyze and assimilate large complex information to quickly identify strategies and solutions for action during rapidly changing conditions.
Theme (college-wide):Writing Use writing to discover, develop and communicate one's own creative and critical ideas, and respond effectively in writing to the spoken, written, and visual ideas of others.	**Authentic Communication** Convey information and deliver messages with transparency and speed, with a variety of media, in a manner that engages the audience and builds bridges between business units.

Figure 21: Samples of Robust Learning Outcome Statements

POG/COG/WOG TITLE: WOG: Aligning Essential Content with Learning Outcomes   **Date:** _____

Concepts & Issues	Skills	Assessment Tasks	Intended Outcomes
What must the learners understand to demonstrate the intended outcome?	*What skills must the learners master to demonstrate the intended outcome?*	*What will learners do in here to demonstrate evidence of the outcome?*	*What do learners need to be able to DO "out there" in the rest of life that we're responsible for "in here"?*
<ul><li>Outcome-based learning</li><li>Designing backwards - outside in</li><li>Real-life roles</li><li>Essential content and lean learning</li><li>Conceptual learning</li><li>Skill development</li><li>Critical thinking</li><li>Issue resolution</li><li>Outcome Guides: COG, POG, WOG</li></ul>	<ul><li>Analyze outcomes for essential concepts, issues and skills.</li><li>Scrutinize large amounts of information and extract essential content based on intended outcomes.</li><li>Organize content in a way that is consistent with how it is actually learned (concepts, skills and issues).</li></ul>	1. Complete the Concept, Issues and Skills portion of a Course Outcome Guide that meets the criteria for alignment and delimitation.	1. Derive essential course content from an analysis of intended learning outcomes. (Design-backward process). 2. Organize course content with regard to how content is actually learned (concepts, skills, issues).
<ul><li>Topics vs Concepts, Skills and Issues</li><li>Information overload and cognitive load</li><li>Loss of topics/content</li></ul>			

What issues must the learners be able to resolve to demonstrate the outcome?

Figure 22: WOG: Aligning Essential Content with Learning Outcomes
Resource: *The CONTENT Primer: Aligning Essential Content with Learning Outcomes*

Scoring Guide for Content Descriptions

Use this rating to assess your Content Descriptions
1=absent   2=developing   3=adequate   4=well developed

Characteristics of Good Content Descriptions	1	2	3	4	Additional comments and specific suggestions for improvement
1. Concepts	1	2	3	4	
Consists of key words or phrases that describe the essential ideas about which the learners must discover some depth of meaning in order to achieve the intended outcomes (8–15 is usually sufficient).					
2. Issues	1	2	3	4	
Consists of the key problems learners must work to resolve, which are inherent in the intended outcomes (usually no more than 4–5).					
3. Skills	1	2	3	4	
Consists of action statements which describe abilities that are essential to demonstrate the intended outcomes (usually no more than 8).					

Figure 23: Scoring Guide for Content Descriptions

POG/COG/WOG TITLE: WOG: Implementing Work Quality Assessment Strategies and Criteria   **Date:** _____

Concepts & Issues	Skills	Assessment Tasks	Intended Outcomes
What must the learners understand to demonstrate the intended outcome?	*What skills must the learners master to demonstrate the intended outcome?*	*What will learners do in here to demonstrate evidence of the outcome?*	*What do learners need to be able to DO "out there" in the rest of life that we're responsible for "in here"?*
• Learning outcomes and learning evidence • Three purposes of learning assessment • Quality work assessment • Assessment tasks vs tests • Direct evidence • Indirect evidence • Kinds of quality assessment tools • Using qualitative and quantitative evidence • Content validity	1. Align assessment tasks with learning outcomes. 2. Identify assessment task(s) that apply to real-life applications. 3. Research quality indicators of assessment tasks from literature. 4. Use an affinity process with colleagues to generate quality assessment criteria. 5. Document assessment tasks and criteria in design documents.	1. Describe how moving to work quality assessment strategies might change what learners currently do to show evidence of course or program outcomes in your discipline/program. 2. Formulate and document quality assessment criteria for a course's or program's assessment task(s).	1. Determine appropriate assessment tasks that align with intended learning outcomes for one's own program or course. 2. Create quality assessment criteria for program and course level assessment tasks in one's own program or course.
• Accountability • Content validity • Instructor work load			

What issues must the learners be able to resolve to demonstrate the outcome?

Figure 24 : WOG: Implementing Work Quality Assessment Strategies and Criteria
Resource: *The ASSESSMENT Primer: Assessing and Tracking Evidence of Learning Outcomes*

Example of Assessment Criteria	
Assessment Criteria	–The following criteria emerged from the process for defining quality criteria in response to the following intended learning outcome.
Learning Outcome	–To engage in collaborative tasks in the workplace, the home and the community in ways that maximize the achievement of shared goals.
Work Task	–Work as a team member on a project.

Theme/Quality Factor	Quality Criteria/Indicators
Individual Responsibility	–Takes responsibility for the work –Shares responsibilities –Knows what she/he is responsible for –Works to the end –Stays engaged
Communication and Information Exchange	–Listens to others' ideas –Contributes own ideas –Keeps everyone informed –Uses technology to stay connected –Provides useful information to others on the team –Listens, withholding immediate judgment
Work Contribution	–Does his/her share of work –Expects others to do their share –Helps identify member strengths and weaknesses –Identifies own strengths and weaknesses
Task Coordination	–Helps clarify team tasks –Helps organize and prioritize work –Helps to keep the work moving
Adaptability	–Is able to make adjustments when necessary –Handles need for change –Can sense the need to change direction
Interdependence	–Trusts others to do their share –Lets others do their share –Connects with others who can help –Respects and uses diverse voices to move the work along –Shares recognition for successes –Shares responsibility for failures

Figure 25: Example of Assessment Criteria

POG/COG/WOG TITLE: WOG: Creating Work Quality Assessment Tools— Checklists, Scoring Guides, and Rubrics   **Date:** _____

Concepts & Issues	Skills	Assessment Tasks	Intended Outcomes
What must the learners understand to demonstrate the intended outcome?	*What skills must the learners master to demonstrate the intended outcome?*	*What will learners do in here to demonstrate evidence of the outcome?*	*What do learners need to be able to DO "out there" in the rest of life that we're responsible for "in here"?*

• Assessment tasks
• Assessment criteria
• Work quality assessment
• Quality factors
• Quality indicators
• Checklists
• Scoring guides
• Rubrics
• Direct evidence
• Indirect evidence
• Assist, advance, adjust
• Assessment tools (See *The ASSESSMENT Primer*)
	1. Distinguish factors from indicators.
	2. Formulate assessment tools using standard templates.
		1. Review and refine assessment criteria.
		2. Draft three different kinds of quality assessment tools that address three different purposes:
		  1. Checklists
		  2. Scoring Guides
		  3. Rubrics
			Prerequisite work session: Implementing Work Quality Assessment Strategies and Criteria
			1. Review and refine work tasks learners will complete to show qualitative evidence of learning outcomes.
			2. Review and refine quality assessment criteria with other professionals to derive quality factors and indicators that can be used to judge learner's work on a given task.
			3. Build a checklist, scoring guide, and rubric from quality assessment criteria.

Establishing validity and reliability

What issues must the learners be able to resolve to demonstrate the outcome?

Figure 26: WOG: Creating Work Quality Assessment Tools—Checklists, Scoring Guides, and Rubrics
Resource: *The ASSESSMENT Primer: Assessing and Tracking Evidence of Learning Outcomes*

Scoring Guide for Assessing Team Work

Name: _____ Project Title _____

Course Name and Number: _____ Start Date: _____ Finish Date: _____

Intended Learning Outcome: Work collaboratively in a team environment, to complete a project, to standards.

Directions: Circle the number that best summarizes your assessment of a team member's performance. Please write suggestions for improvement on the back of the page for any of the indicators you rated "0" to "3". Calculate an average for each indicator and provide an average of the total.

	Absent	Developing	Adequate	Well Developed	
1. Communication and Information Exchange					
• Withheld judgment while listening to others	0	1 2 3	4 5 6	7 8 9	NA
• Encouraged and valued the contribution of all members	0	1 2 3	4 5 6	7 8 9	NA
• Enhanced the flow of information to all members	0	1 2 3	4 5 6	7 8 9	NA
• Expressed and advocated for own ideas	0	1 2 3	4 5 6	7 8 9	NA
• Used technology to stay connected	0	1 2 3	4 5 6	7 8 9	NA

Average ☐

2. Work Contribution					
• Engaged willingly in the work	0	1 2 3	4 5 6	7 8 9	NA
• Contributed to development of ground rules	0	1 2 3	4 5 6	7 8 9	NA
• Provided useful information and experience	0	1 2 3	4 5 6	7 8 9	NA
• Willingly gave and received constructive feeback	0	1 2 3	4 5 6	7 8 9	NA

Average ☐

3. Task Coordination					
• Helped clarify team's task(s)	0	1 2 3	4 5 6	7 8 9	NA
• Helped organize and chart work flow	0	1 2 3	4 5 6	7 8 9	NA
• Contributed to efficient use of team time	0	1 2 3	4 5 6	7 8 9	NA

Average ☐

4. Individual Responsibility					
• Asked for verification of individual responsibilities	0	1 2 3	4 5 6	7 8 9	NA
• Advocated for needs to do the job	0	1 2 3	4 5 6	7 8 9	NA
• Assumed responsibilities	0	1 2 3	4 5 6	7 8 9	NA
• Stayed engaged until the team's task(s) was finished	0	1 2 3	4 5 6	7 8 9	NA
• Followed team's timelines and deadlines	0	1 2 3	4 5 6	7 8 9	NA

Average ☐

5. Adaptability					
• Showed respect for members' differences in ability and work style	0	1 2 3	4 5 6	7 8 9	NA
• Adapted to change	0	1 2 3	4 5 6	7 8 9	NA
• Reflected on team's process and interaction	0	1 2 3	4 5 6	7 8 9	NA

Average ☐

6. Interdependence					
• Helped build internal and external networks to get the work done	0	1 2 3	4 5 6	7 8 9	NA
• Looked for "intersections" where diverse voices united the efforts	0	1 2 3	4 5 6	7 8 9	NA
• Helped synthesize input	0	1 2 3	4 5 6	7 8 9	NA
• Assisted other team members	0	1 2 3	4 5 6	7 8 9	NA
• Trusted other team members	0	1 2 3	4 5 6	7 8 9	NA

Average ☐

Check one: ☐ Self-assessment
☐ Peer Assessment by _____
☐ Instructor Assessment by_____

Average Score: _____

Figure 27: Scoring Guide for Assessing Team Work

POG/COG/WOG TITLE: WOG: Mapping the Learners' Journey

Date: _____

Concepts & Issues

What must the learners understand to demonstrate the intended outcome?

- Program vs departments
- Program map
- Three levels of outcomes
- Mapping conventions
- Real-life roles
- Entry requirements
- Intended learning outcomes
- Learner's journey
- Common flow patterns
- Integrated experiences
- Key and capstone assessments
- Evolution of program maps

- Willingness to participate/collaborate
- Issue resolution through consensus
- Resistance to change
- Question reluctance

What issues must the learners be able to resolve to demonstrate the outcome?

Skills

What skills must the learners master to demonstrate the intended outcome?

1. Use mapping conventions.
2. Think systemically.
3. Use inquiry to evoke key points in mapping a learner's journey in courses and programs.
4. Collaborate and build consensus on key issues in mapping a learner's journey.
5. Focus on intended learning outcomes.

Assessment Tasks

What will learners do in here to demonstrate evidence of the outcome?

1. Working with other colleagues in your program, create a first generation program map that reveals:
   - how courses are aligned with the intended outcomes,
   - in which courses evidence of learning outcomes is collected and
   - what issues need to be addressed to improve the learning experience in this program.
2. Produce an Emerging Issues List along with next steps.

Intended Outcomes

What do learners need to be able to DO "out there" in the rest of life that we're responsible for "in here"?

1. Create a visual map of the learner's journey through an academic or training program.
2. Examine the learner's journey; identify and document emerging issues that could improve learning outcomes.

Figure 28: WOG : Mapping the Learners' Journey
Resource: *The MAPPING Primer: Mapping the Way to Learning Outcomes*

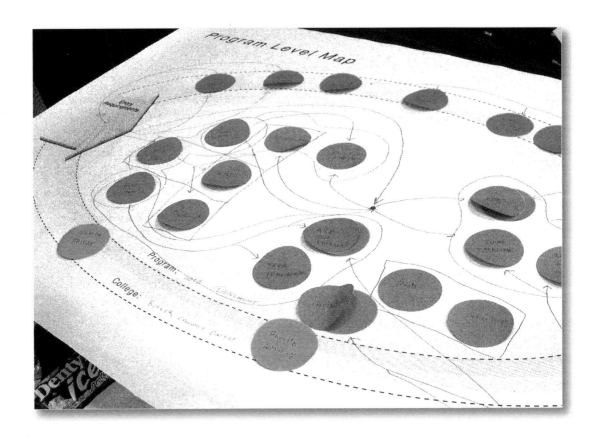

Figure 29: First Generation Program Map

POG/COG/WOG TITLE: ___WOG: Mapping Programs—Reviewing Second___ **Date:** _____
Generation Maps

Concepts & Issues	Skills	Assessment Tasks	Intended Outcomes
What must the learners understand to demonstrate the intended outcome?	*What skills must the learners master to demonstrate the intended outcome?*	*What will learners do in here to demonstrate evidence of the outcome?*	*What do learners need to be able to DO "out there" in the rest of life that we're responsible for "in here"?*
• Entry requirements • Intended roles • Intended learning outcomes • Course learning experiences • Key assessments • Capstone assessment • Sequencing of learning experiences • Connections/interdependencies • Integration of learning • Use of external learning • Backup and redundancy (See details in Figure 32, of *The MAPPING Primer*)	1. Critical thinking. 2. Systemic thinking.	1. Work with colleagues to reconstruct the first draft of a program map until it meets the quality criteria for program maps. 2. Do a walk-through of the map with other instructional staff and address their questions.	Modify and enhance the first draft of a program map until it clearly depicts the alignment of learning experiences with the program learning outcomes.
Negotiating changes in the program Territory/ownership			

What issues must the learners be able to resolve to demonstrate the outcome?

Figure 30: WOG : Mapping Programs—Reviewing Second Generation Program Maps
Resource: *The MAPPING Primer: Mapping the Way to Learning Outcomes*

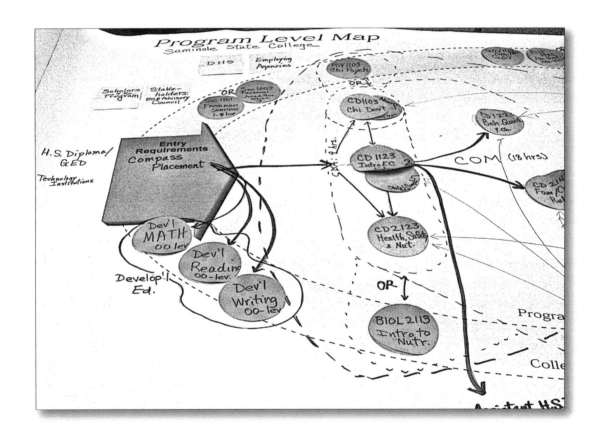

Figure 31: Second Generation Program Map

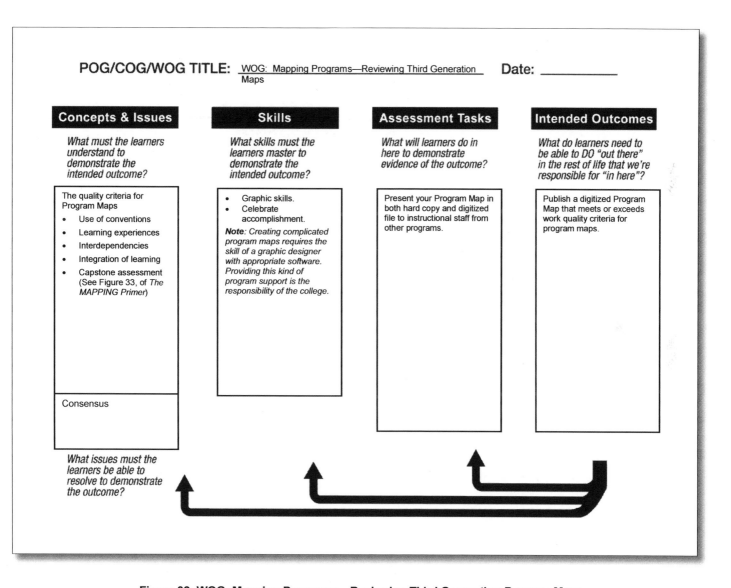

POG/COG/WOG TITLE: WOG: Mapping Programs—Reviewing Third Generation Maps   **Date:** _____

Concepts & Issues

What must the learners understand to demonstrate the intended outcome?

The quality criteria for Program Maps
- Use of conventions
- Learning experiences
- Interdependencies
- Integration of learning
- Capstone assessment (See Figure 33, of *The MAPPING Primer*)

Consensus

What issues must the learners be able to resolve to demonstrate the outcome?

Skills

What skills must the learners master to demonstrate the intended outcome?

- Graphic skills.
- Celebrate accomplishment.

Note: *Creating complicated program maps requires the skill of a graphic designer with appropriate software. Providing this kind of program support is the responsibility of the college.*

Assessment Tasks

What will learners do in here to demonstrate evidence of the outcome?

Present your Program Map in both hard copy and digitized file to instructional staff from other programs.

Intended Outcomes

What do learners need to be able to DO "out there" in the rest of life that we're responsible for "in here"?

Publish a digitized Program Map that meets or exceeds work quality criteria for program maps.

Figure 32: WOG: Mapping Programs—Reviewing Third Generation Program Maps
Resource: *The MAPPING Primer: Mapping the Way to Learning Outcomes*

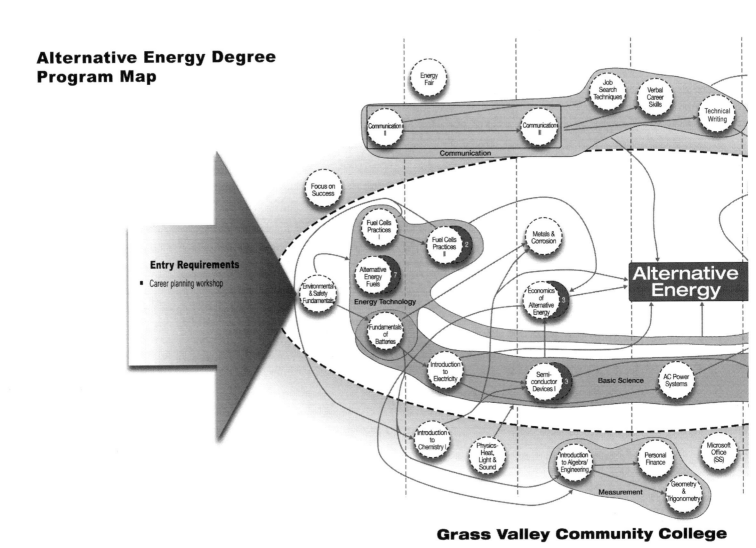

Figure 33: Third Generation Program Map

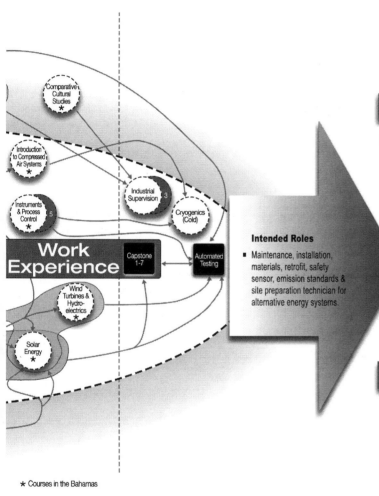

★ Courses in the Bahamas

Intended Roles

- Maintenance, installation, materials, retrofit, safety sensor, emission standards & site preparation technician for alternative energy systems.

INTENDED LEARNING OUTCOMES

1. Demonstrate effective verbal and written communication skills as an individual and as a team member.

2. Demonstrate basic electrical, mechanical, chemical, mathematical and computer skills involved in maintaining alternative energy systems.

3. Apply sound business and economic principles to achieve and maintain profitability of alternative energy systems.

4. Follow quality and safety procedures.

5. Install, repair and design alternative energy systems.

6. Fabricate and test prototypes.

7. Participate in researching current and emerging alternative energy systems.

ORGANIZATION-WIDE LEARNING OUTCOMES

- Communicate effectively
- Think critically
- Practice from a code of ethics
- Interact well with others
- Show evidence of cultural and global awareness

POG/COG/WOG TITLE: WOG: Eight Essential Guiding Practices for Instructors   **Date:** _____

Concepts & Issues

What must the learners understand to demonstrate the intended outcome?

- Guiding vs teaching
- Learner centered
- Intended learning outcomes
- Essential content
- Assessment tasks and assignments
- Alignment of outcomes, content and assessment tasks
- Learning community
- Assess to *assist*
- Assess to *advance*
- Assess to *adjust*
- Assessment tools
- Proficiency
- Reflection

Note: Each of these concepts are discussed at length in The GUIDING Primer.

- Old teaching methods
- Content driven curriculum
- Accountability for results
- Fear of change
- Time to learn and apply new skills and shift paradigms

What issues must the learners be able to resolve to demonstrate the outcome?

Skills

What skills must the learners master to demonstrate the intended outcome?

1. Focusing on outcomes.
2. Creating essential content and assessment tasks.
3. Building community.
4. Assessing to *assist*.
5. Building proficiency.
6. Reflecting on issues.
7. Using evidence to *advance* learners.
8. Gathering, displaying and using evidence to *adjust* the learning experience.

Assessment Tasks

What will learners do in here to demonstrate evidence of the outcome?

1. Develop a plan to build a community of learners in a course.
2. Determine learning strategies and sequence to build proficiency that is aligned with learning outcome(s).
3. Assess your application of eight essential guiding practices and create a development plan.
4. Assess learners' work to assist learners and provide feedback to meet learning outcomes.
5. Develop an activity map for a course.
6. Review assessment results for course outcomes and develop an action plan for making course changes and adjustments.

Intended Outcomes

What do learners need to be able to DO "out there" in the rest of life that we're responsible for "in here"?

Move beyond the old perception of what it means to teach to guiding learning in pursuit of intended learning outcomes.

Figure 34: WOG: Eight Essential Guiding Practices for Instructors
Resource: *The GUIDING Primer: Guiding Toward Learning Outcomes*

Template: Building Community Tool

Directions: In preparing for a specific course, reflect on the following questions and document the specific things you plan to do during the course in the interest of establishing a sense of community.

BELONGING

Question: What will I do to create a sense of belonging at the very start of my course?	Conduct a "warm-up" team activity: what they "know," need to "know," want to "know."
Questions: What will I do to sustain the sense of community throughout the course?	Learners work in teams on class projects.

VISIONING

Question: How will I share the full picture of the journey we are undertaking together?	Share a COG and Course Map and review periodically.

ENGAGING

Question: What activities will I plan that will actively engage them with each other?	Learners, in teams of three, conduct lab experiments in the main areas: solar, wind, and fuel cells
Questions: In what specific activities will I engage myself as a member of the community?	Model and demonstrate each lab experiment prior to learners engaging in experimental assignments.

Figure 35: Building Community Tool (page 1 of 2)

Template: Community Building Tool

CARING

Question:	
In what different ways will I communicate that I care about them?	Provide praise and positive feedback of learner performance; welcome learners at each class.

RESPECTING

Question:	
What will I do to show respect for all members of our community?	Encourage creativity and diversity in learners' work tasks; use scoring guides to assess.

SHARING RESPONSIBILITY

Question:	
What will I do to find out if members of the community feel I have carried out my specific responsibilities to them?	Ask learners to assess my teaching performance.
Questions: How will I help them understand their own responsibility to themselves and their work teams?	Discuss joint responsibility for achieving outcomes.

Figure 35: Building Community Tool (page 2 of 2)

Facilitator Training

We acknowledged earlier that one of the best things any college can do to sustain a learning outcomes and assessment system college-wide is to train a group of in-house facilitators to lead the re-occurring work sessions. Remember, each work session is not a single event but rather an on-going cycle that keeps the system advancing, and requires the services of a number of facilitators over time. Maintaining a core of in-house facilitators should be a priority. Training facilitators is most often done by bringing in an expert trainer such as the Outcome Strategists associated with this series. For more information, go to *www.outcomeprimers.com*.

Facilitator Training
(3–9 hours)

1. Facilitating the development of robust learning outcomes at the program, course and organization levels.

2. Facilitating the creation of program maps to show the alignment of courses and assessments with intended learning outcomes.

3. Facilitating the development of work quality assessment criteria and different kinds of assessment tools.

Focused Conversations

Just getting leaders and instructors engaged in a *conversation* focused on specific issues around outcomes and assessment goes a long way to keeping the agenda moving forward. This *SUS-*

TAINABILITY Primer has raised four primary issues around which these conversations can be focused. But many other issues will emerge when you and others work through the Sustainability Tools in PART TWO. Be careful not to try to tackle too many too quickly.

And, keep in mind, these conversations are not work sessions or trainings—they are *conversations* that last about an hour or so and are continued or repeated as long as interest is sustained and issues persist.

Conversations on Sustaining the Outcomes and Assessment Initiative

1. Leadership, trust, and successsion planning
2. Support for professional development
3. How to involve instructors
4. How to integrate curricular systems

Summary

The development and sustainability of learning outcomes and assessment in colleges today is deeply contingent on what we do internally to prepare our leaders and instructors in new curricular design processes.

In PART FIVE of this Primer, we have outlined a series of eight core work sessions, three facilitator trainings, and four focused conversations that form a complete professional development plan for learning outcomes and assessment that keeps a college moving forward. It's an essential part that sustains the system and keeps it working over time.

PART SIX

Creating and Sustaining an Outcomes and Assessment System through System Integration

A complex system that works is invariably found to have evolved from a simple system that worked.

—John Gall

Creating and Sustaining an Outcomes and Assessment System through System Integration

A Systems View

> **System:** *A network of interdependent parts that serve a common purpose.*
>
> **Outcomes and Assessment System:** *A network of curriculum design and approval, learning assessment, professional development, and program review processes that assures the continuous improvement of experiences for the learners we serve.*
>
> **System Integration:** *The efficient flow of ideas, energy and information among the different, interdependent parts of a single system.*

System integration is the one factor that we seem to know the least about and see the least evidence of in an outcomes and assessment system. And yet, the success of all our efforts hinges on this one thing—*the recognition that the four processes of curriculum design and approval, learning assessment, professional development, and program review are interdependent parts of an outcome and assessment system.* These four processes need to function as an integrated system. Failing to recognize the importance of system integration is a huge issue in college cultures that are overly compartmentalized and *committeeized. So, let's go back and put this all in context.*

Background

Thinking and reading about systems theory, out of context, can be overwhelming. Just read what John Gall (1975) says about systems in his book *Systematics*:

> *Everything is a system.... Everything is part of a larger system.... Everything in the universe is infinitely systematizable, both upwards downwards...all systems are infinitely complex.*

Wow! We're not sure that helps very much, so let's put it in context where it might make more sense.

We all recognize that a college is a system that's made up of many parts. The biggest parts take one of two different forms. They are either core systems of the college or support systems of the college. Whether core or support, they are both made up of many different processes that function together to sustain the larger system.

Core systems: Core systems are at the very center of the organization's mission. It is probably safe to assume that the curricular offerings are the reason the college exists—to serve the intellectual needs of the learners. This means that an outcomes and assessment system is one of the core systems of every college.

Support systems: These systems provide support to ensure the organization is running efficiently. Think of things like technology, business and accounting, facilities, human resources, housing. They exist to support the core college systems.

Integrated processes: Beyond these two forms of systems in a college, there are much smaller sub-systems, or integrated processes, that are brought together to function as a coordinated whole around a specific purpose.

So, what does it mean to function as a system? To put it as simply as possible, it means to work toward a common purpose through fine-tuned relationships and networks. It means working interdependently, as a whole entity, with identifiable inputs and outputs.

In Figure 36, Four Core Processes in a College Outcomes and Assessment System, shown on page 127, we have illustrated how we see an outcomes and assessment system functioning as one of the college's core systems, composed of four primary processes: curriculum design and approval, learning assessment, professional development, and program review. Each is shown as a dynamic cycle of activity that continuously informs each of the other processes. The image gives us the feeling that each part constantly re-*creates* each of the other parts in a dynamic dance—all in the context of an ever-changing college—the larger dance.

This image of interdependency is not as common in colleges as we would hope. The more common image continues to be the silo—department and committees that fail to talk to each other, go their own ways, duplicate tasks, and defend their territories. In essence, committees fail to function as a connected system because they fail to see the larger purpose that connects them.

Here is a scenario from one specific college that illustrates the lack of system integration. If it be known, the same story has been repeated over and again in other colleges when institutions do not have a systems view of outcomes and assessment.

Scenario: As both a college administrator and an outcomes strategist, I (Kathy) have been involved with the assessment efforts for a number of different colleges. I watched one college for over a period of ten years react at critical times to deal with assessment concerns. Their pattern was one of appointing a different person or committee each time to conduct an assessment activity or event. On at least one occasion, I was the event; they brought me in to conduct a work session. But when the activity was completed, the committee was disbanded, the results were reported, and assessment faded from institutional memory. It was an event with no real connection and no cycle.

(NOTE: You may want to review PART ONE of this Primer where we graphically illustrated how outcomes and assessment efforts cycle and mature.)

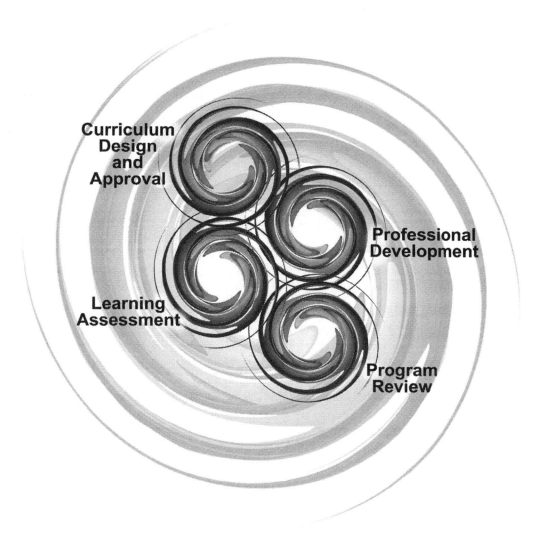

Figure 36: Four Core Curricular Processes in a College Outcomes and Assessment System

Stages of Integration and System Maturity

The Higher Learning Commission recognizes four different stages of maturing in process and results as illustrated in Figure 37, Stages in Systems Maturity: Processes and Figure 38: Stages of Systems Maturity: Results, on the following pages.

Using Figures 37 and 38, an outcomes and assessment system would then be described as moving and maturing in terms beginning with being *reactive* to being *systematic*, followed by being *aligned* and *integrated*. We have included these tables for you to examine and further use as conversation starters with administrators and faculty leaders. *Before reading on, take some time here to reflect on which description best* describes the current state of your organization's outcomes and assessment system (*reacting, systematic, aligned, integrated*) for both processes and results.

Stages in System Maturity: Processes			
Reacting	**Systematic**	**Aligned**	**Integrated**
The institution focuses on activities and initiatives that respond to immediate needs or problems rather than anticipating future requirements, capacities, or changes. Goals are implicit and poorly defined. Informal procedures and habits account for all but the most formal aspects of institutional operations.	The institution is beginning to operate via generally understood, repeatable, and often documented processes and is prone to make the goal of most activities explicit, measurable, and subject to improvement. Institutional silos are eroding and signs of coordination and the implementation of effective practices across units are evident. Institutional goals are generally understood.	The institution operates according to processes that are explicit, repeatable, and periodically evaluated for improvement. Processes address key goals and strategies, and lessons learned are shared among insitiutional units. Coordination and communication among units is emphasized so stakeholders relate what they do to institutional goals and strategies.	Operations are characterized by explicit, predictable processes that are repeatable and regularly evaluated for optimum effectiveness. Efficiencies across units are achieved through analysis, transparency, innovation, and sharing. Processes and measures track progress on key strategic and operational goals. Outsiders request permission to visit and study why the institution is so successful.

Adapted from *Baldrige Excellence Framework: A Systems Approach to Improving Your Organization's Performance (Education)* by The Higher Learning Commission. (April 2015. Source: AQIP Pathway Systems Appraisal: A Resource for Peer Reviewers)

Figure 37: Stages in System Maturity: Processes

Stages in System Maturity: Results			
Reacting	**Systematic**	**Aligned**	**Integrated**
Activities, initiatives, and operational processes may not generate data or the data is not collected, aggregated, or analyzed. Institutional goals lack measures, metrics, and/or benchmarks for evaluating progress. The monitoring of quality of operational practices and procedures may be based on assumptions about quality. Data collected may not be segmented or distributed effectively to inform decision-making.	Data and information are collected and archived for use, available to evaluate progress, and are analyzed at various levels. The results are shared and begin to erode institutional silos and foster improvement initiatives across institutional units. The tracking of performance on institutional goals has begun in a manner that yields trend data and lends itself to comparative measures in some areas.	Measures, metrics, and benchmarks are understood and used by all relevant stakeholders. Good performance levels are reported with beneficial trends sustained over time in many areas of importance. Results are segmented and distributed to all responsible institutional units in a manner that supports effective decision-making, planning, and collaboration on improvement initiatives. Measures and metrics are designed to enable the aggregation and analysis of results at an institutional level.	Data and information are analyzed and used to optimize operations on an ongoing basis. Performance levels are monitored using appropriate benchmarks. Trend data has been accrued and analyzed for most areas of performance. Results are shared, aggregated, segmented, and analyzed in a manner that supports transparency, efficiency, collaboration, and progress on organizational goals. Measures and metrics for strategic and operational goals yield results that are used in decision-making and resource allocations.

Adapted from *Baldrige Excellence Framework: A Systems Approach to Improving Your Organization's Performance (Education)* by The Higher Learning Commission. (April 2015, Source AQIP Pathway Systems Appraisal: A Resource for Peer Reviewers)

Figure 38: Stages in System Maturity: Results

The Integration of Core Curricular Processes

We earlier defined core systems as systems that are at the very center of the organization's mission; the reason it exists—Outcomes and Assessment being one of those core systems. Within that system are the four core curricular processes we identified earlier: curriculum design and approval, learning assessment, professional development, and program review. Each of these processes functions quite independently in many colleges, which greatly limits their effectiveness. They work together more efficiently as one integrated system.

As we look at each of these processes in some detail, we need to keep in mind that the development of curriculum does not originate in a committee, an academic department or even the college; it originates with advisory committees, accrediting bodies, professional associations, and the needs of the national and global community—the larger system we serve.

Curriculum Design and Approval Processes

Curriculum design and approval is a process for creating and approving courses and programs, managing and tracking the curriculum as it moves through the approval process, as well as storing, retrieving, and reporting information to other units.

Additions and changes in curricular offerings by the college are usually initiated and designed at the program level and include three primary design steps:

1) envisioning, defining, and aligning the learning outcomes at the course, program, and organization level,

2) identifying those specific assessment tasks that provide learners with the best way to show evidence of the learning outcomes, and

3) deconstructing the content so that only the content that is essential to the intended

learning outcomes (concepts, issues, and skills) is included.

Every college has its own format for curriculum design and many of those remain content-focused rather that outcome-focused. In an outcome-based system, we recommend using a format that clearly shows the alignment of content and assessment with intended outcomes, such as the Course Outcome Guide (COG) and a Program Outcome Guide (POG). (For examples of the outcomes format, look again at PART FIVE where we include a series of Work Session Outcome Guides—*WOGS*—in the identical format.) Colleges who use these templates refer to the curricular design process as ***cogging and pogging.***

The design of a program map, when added to a POG/COG/WOG, visually depicts how learners move through the curriculum—how courses are sequenced to best enable learners to realize the intended outcomes. In ad-

dition, these templates and maps are extremely helpful to both instructors and approval committees showing the essential content and flow of a course or program. Figure 4: Alternative Energy Degree Program (shown earlier on pages 14–15) is an example of a program map. Other Program Maps are illustrated in *The MAPPING Primer: Mapping the Way to Learning Outcomes*, a companion book in this series.

In most colleges, curriculum design proposals must be reviewed and approved both by the department and a college-wide committee. The approval processes are usually well established and carefully documented.

The output of the approval process is an official college document, stored and easily accessible to administrators, instructors and learners. These documents provide input to the college catalog, advising materials, college's information system and its websites.

We have been known to say that when the approval process is mature, it should be like UPS—anyone should be able to pinpoint exactly where a piece of curriculum is in the approval process, how long it has been there and what's holding it up—and when it's likely to be approved. The steps involved in the approval processes are unique to every college.

Here are the essential questions that drive the curriculum design and approval processes.

Questions that Drive the Curriculum Design and Approval Processes:

What do learners need to be able to do "out there" that we are responsible for "in here?"

What will learners do "in here" to demonstrate evidence of the learning outcome(s)?

What concepts and skills must the learners understand and develop to demonstrate the learning outcome(s)?

What issues must learners be able to resolve?

Approval:

Does the curriculum meet established criteria?

Learning Assessment Processes

Learning assessment involves processes for collecting, storing, scoring, aggregating, analyzing, and using evidence of learning to regularly improve programs and courses. These processes are driven by learning outcomes at three different levels: organization-wide, program, and course (multi section). Processes differ at each level.

We need to make one distinction before we move on. When we talk about a system for aggregating data to study and improve our own practices, we are not talking about daily evaluation of a learner's work; we are talking about aggregating direct and indirect learning evidence at the course, program and organization levels to determine what we are doing well and not so well. Establishing processes at three different levels requires strategic planning for processes scheduled over several years.

The input to assessment processes are the curricular documents approved in the curriculum design process, work quality standards (factors and indicators), selected artifacts of learner work, testing data and other indirect evidence that provides insights into the strengths and weaknesses of programs and courses.

The output of each assessment process is usually a report that summarizes the results of the data using charts and narratives, but it is the data that generates the conversation and subsequent change.

When data pertains to a course with multiple sections, the data will drive a rich conversation among instructors who teach the same course. When the data is at the program level, all the instructors who teach program courses should be involved in the dialogue. When the data pertains to organization-wide learning outcomes, the conversation is bigger and broader with all programs across the college involved. In the end, it's the conversation and instructors that improve the system.

Each of the assessment processes we have just described operates on different cycles. While systems evolve over time, so also do processes. When processes are new in a system-wide effort, they are usually just *reactive* while everyone tries to figure things out. The system evolves and matures over time by establishing firm connections and process cycles.

Cycle: A cycle exists whenever the output of a process becomes one of the inputs in the next cycle. Without a cycle, there is no system; there is only an event.

The organization-wide learning outcomes assessment cycle depends on how many organization-wide outcomes a college defines and how many it could realistically assess in a year. Remember, the process involves not only the gathering and tracking of evidence, but making adjustments to the design, development, or delivery of learning based on the findings and re-assessments after the changes are made. This last part of the process is no small thing and is often referred to as *closing the loop*.

Scenario: If a college has just three organization-wide outcomes (e.g. Communication, Critical Thinking and Cultural Awareness), they might decide to assess one outcome each year with a cycle of three years as shown in Figure 39: Assessment Cycle for Organization-wide Learning Outcomes.

Assessment of Organization-wide Learning Outcomes	Assess	Adjust	Confirm/ Re-assess
Communication	Year 1	Year 2	Year 3
Critical Thinking	Year 2	Year 3	Year 4
Culture Awareness	Year 3	Year 4	Year 5

Figure 39: Assessment Cycle for Organization-wide Learning Outcomes

Determining an appropriate cycle for program assessment would be similar. Instructors who teach in a given program would determine how many program outcomes could be assessed each year and moved through the complete cycle. The cycle schedule would also be subject to when courses are taught and artifacts can be gathered. A typical five-year assessment cycle at the program level is shown in Figure 40: Assessment Cycle for Program Learning Outcomes.

Assessment of Program Learning Outcomes	Assess	Adjust	Confirm/ Re-assess
Program Outcome 1 Course G Course J	Year 1	Year 2	Year 3
Program Outcome 2 Course C Course F	Year 1	Year 2	Year 3
Program Outcome 3 Course A Course H	Year 2	Year 3	Year 4
Program Outcome 4 Course B Course K	Year 2	Year 3	Year 4
Program Outcome 5 Course D Course J	Year 3	Year 4	Year 5
Program Outcome 6 Course E Course I	Year 3	Year 4	Year 5
Organization-wide LOA survey	Year 1	Year 2	Year 3

Figure 40: Assessment Cycle for Program Learning Outcomes

Earlier, we talked about preparing a *program map* as part of the curriculum design process at the program level. We referred you to Figure 4 (pages 14–15), Alternative Energy Degree Program, as an example of a program map that includes capstone assessment points. The assessment points are annotated on the map by the circle (a course) and indicating the number of the program outcome that will be assessed in this course.

In the same figure, we see courses in Industrial Supervision, Economics of Alternative Energy, and the Semi-conductor Device where instructors determine how well learners are achieving the third program outcome and what adjustments, if any, are needed in those courses. While the program's capstone course focuses on the program outcomes, it often provides the opportunity to collect evidence of organization-wide learning outcomes as well. This is the kind of planning we should expect when a system is fully integrated.

When we think about the multi-section courses, we needn't assume that it is necessary to collect evidence from every section of every course. Instead, we need to focus our efforts on those courses that have the most influence on the whole system (i.e. prerequisites, gate keepers, developmental courses, or those identified as a potential issue by a course later in the sequence).

Example: Here is an example of a plan for two required English courses (English 100 and 101) that are used by the majority of programs in the college, as shown in Figure 41: Assessment Cycle of Learning Outcomes for ENG-100, ENG-101. Because these courses focus on an organization-wide communications outcome and more contextual communication outcomes at the program level, it makes strategic sense to collect learning evidence in the interest of strengthening the courses. After all, they have the potential to affect the greatest number of learners.

Assessment Cycle for Learning Outcomes of ENG-100, ENG-101	Assess	Adjust	Confirm/ Re-assess
ENG-100	Year 1	Year 2	Year 3
ENG-101	Year 3	Year 4	Year 5

Figure 41: Assessment Cycle of Learning Outcomes for ENG-100, ENG-101

The processes for assessing learning outcomes that we have described above all hinges on asking the right questions. Here are the essential questions that drive the processes at every level:

Questions that Drive the Learning Assessment Processes

1. What kinds of direct and indirect evidence of learning will be collected? When and where will it be collected?

2. Who will be involved in an analysis of the data?

3. Who and how will we report the finding?

4. What are the benchmarks and the criteria we will apply?

5. What does the evidence tell us?

6. What adjustments should we make to improve

---

learning experiences in this course/program based on the evidence we have collected?

7. What adjustments can we make to ensure the assessment processes are more effective and efficient?

8. How can we best use the evidence we have?

9. When should the next assessment be scheduled?

Program Review Processes

At first, it might appear that what we have described as *learning assessment* is the same thing we are now calling *program review*. Be assured—it isn't. There is a substantial difference:

Learning assessment is about knowing the extent to which the learners have met the intended learning outcomes; *program review* seeks to determine the continued relevance of the program - what is needed to maintain or expand the program, as well as determine when it should be discontinued. A *program review* cycle is usually between 3 and 7 years.

Scenario 1: Until rather recently, one college we visited had a program in Information Technology designed to prepare graduates to work on mainframe computers. The courses in this program were only offered periodically due to low enrollment, but no one wanted to delete the program or even ask the question, "Is this program still relevant?" An assessment of learning outcomes might have revealed evidence that those who did take the courses met or exceeded the expected learning outcomes, but it would not have revealed whether the program remained relevant in the technical world; program review processes would have directly addressed the issue of relevance.

Here's a scenario of what one new leader did to improve the *program review* processes and ensure it was integrated with other related processes.

Scenario 2: A newly appointed Provost, in a mid-west community college, saw a need to review the college's Program Review process to make sure it was aligned with the Master Academic Plan and the Strategic Plan of the College.

Under her leadership, the faculty and staff were able to create new *program review* processes that involved focusing on one theme (student success, partnerships, financial, curriculum, strategic planning) each year in a five-year cycle. This shift was intended to make the work manageable, more focused, and sustainable.

They also integrated it with the program's learning outcomes and assessment and their organization-wide assessments by including them in the year where curriculum was the focus. In addition, they made changes to who would be involved. Instead of reporting the results of the *program review* to an academic council, they moved to a peer review cohort model in order to provide peer discussion and feedback. This kind of change required a committed leader, instructor involvement, collaboration, and mutual trust.

The input needed for program review usually includes enrollment and graduation data, relevant demographics, projected enrollment, evidence of learning, plans for program adjustments, and evidence of progress on planned changes.

The output of program review usually takes the form of a self-study report and agreed-upon next steps including adjustments in the allocation of resources for the program.

Here are the questions that focus the program review processes:

Questions that Drive the Program Review Processes

1. Is the program still relevant and current?

2. How is assessment data (program and organization-wide) used to make informed decisions and improvements?

3. Does the program have appropriate resources (faculty, financial, supplies)?

4. Is the program cost effective and financially viable?

5. How are the instructors involved in planning and design, assessment, decision-making, and curriculum changes?

6. What is the plan for growth and improvement?

Professional Development Processes

When instructors are hired for their expertise in subject matter, why do we just assume they have the expertise to design and sustain an outcomes and assessment system? We can't!

Of the four core curricular processes we illustrated earlier in Figure 36, page 127, *professional development* is the one that produces the *energy* and the institution's internal *capacity* to build and sustain an outcomes and assessment system. This is because it's the people, always the people, who design the system, launch the system, operate the system, and monitor the system in support of the learner and learning.

In an outcomes and assessment system, *professional development* is for all—all instructors, all staff, all administrators (yes even the provost and academic deans), advisory groups, stakeholders, and learners.

All curriculum work is an intensely human process with all its variances and relational challenges. It's the very thing that makes it dynamic and unpredictable at times. But it also means that roles need to be clearly defined to maximize the use of time, energy, and talent. It also means professional development opportunities should align with the role definitions.

Role Definitions

There is a critical balance to be achieved in defining roles within an outcomes and assessment system—a balance between rigidly imposed roles and the total lack of defined roles. Roles should be clear but not rigid. This means everyone needs to know how the various processes interact and be clear about their own responsibilities in carrying out the work of the whole system.

Scenario: Early in my career in higher education, I (Kathy) was asked to lead a taskforce assigned to analyze the Curriculum Design and Approval process to see if approval time could be shortened. As part of our analysis, we interviewed instructors who had recently submitted a curricular design proposal for approval.

To understand their experience, we mapped the approval process, step by step. We identified who was involved in each step and the value they added. It quickly became clear that there was a duplication of work while other tasks went undone. This insight led the taskforce to more carefully define both the process and roles so that the process was more predictable with an annual cycle, deadlines and guarantees. The cycle time for approval became explicit, trackable, transparent, and shorter.

Figure 42, Key Roles Involved in Learning Outcomes and Assessment, is an example of a document that defines the different roles in an outcomes and assessment system. It's the first step in creating a focused professional development plan, which we described in detail in PART FIVE of this Primer.

Roles	Responsibilities
President	Communicates the vision for learning, champions involvement in outcome-based education and assessment.
Vice President of Academic Affairs	Provides proactive leadership to continually improve and ensure sustainability of an outcome and assessment system.
Dean	Advocates for or provides support to instructors in their efforts to develop outcome-based curriculum and learning assessment: involved in curriculum and assessment processes and their improvement.
Department Chair & Program Coordinator	Participates in program assessment and program review.
Director of Curriculum & Chair, Curriculum Committee	Provides leadership and support to design, implement and improve outcome-based curriculum processes. Reports status of curriculum and ensures integration with other related curricular processes; ensures a shared understanding of outcome-based curriculum and that only outcome-based curriculum is approved. Works with Director of Assessment to improve its processes and the integration with other related curricular processes in the Outcome and Assessment System.
Director of Assessment & Chair, Assessment Committee	Provides leadership and support to design, implement and improve assessment processes. Reports assessment results and ensures integration with other related curricular processes; Ensures a shared understanding of assessment. Works with the Director of Curriculum to continually improve its processes and the integration with other related curricular processes in the Outcome and Assessment System.
Professional Development Coordinator	Provides training on defining, assessing, and improving outcomes. For instructional areas, the focus is on learning outcomes and for non-instructional areas, the focus is on operational outcomes.
Instructional Designer	Works with instructors to design and develop outcome-based curriculum and effective assessments that will align with learning outcomes at the course, program and organization-wide levels.
Instructional Technologist	Works with instructors to determine appropriate technology and coach/train in its use to develop learning content.
Instructor (Full/Part Time)	Develops outcome-based curriculum and effective assessments to measure learning outcomes. Collaborates with others to assess learning, interpret results and determine adjustments needed. Provides feedback to learners.
Learner	Actively engages in all aspects of the educational journey (including co-curricular). Provides feedback to instructors, programs, and the college.

Figure 42: Key Roles Involved in Learning Outcomes and Assessment

Support Functions in an Outcomes and Assessment System

According to Webster, *support* is defined as *providing assistance to someone or something to enable them to function in a defined role.* Figure 43, Four Support Functions in an Integrated Outcomes and Assessment System, on the following page, illustrates four major support functions that are essential in an integrated outcomes and assessment system. This illustration is our best effort to show the dynamic, interdependent relationship that exists between the four major processes and the support functions in a mature outcomes and assessment system. The cycling movement in this graphic reminds us that nothing is static in this work; the constant cycling of information, data and feedback loops energizes and sustains the system.

Design Support

Ten years ago, few colleges saw any need for hiring people who called themselves instructional designers; surely, faculty were all instructional designers. Then, with the advent of on-line learning, many colleges found hiring professional designers to be a necessary thing, especially for their technical expertise. But, rarely were even instructional designers better prepared than most instructors to design courses and assessment instruments from an outcomes and assessment perspective. Much of this lack of preparation is due to the lack of an outcome-based framework in graduate programs that prepare instructional designers.

Documentation Support

Documentation support means that all the resources in an outcome and assessment system are readily accessible, centrally located, consistently used, and routinely updated. It includes all the

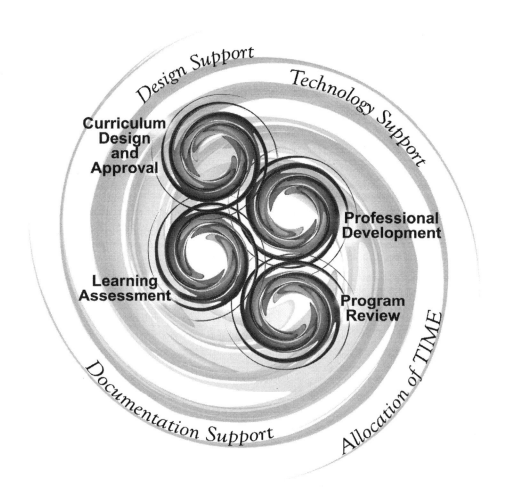

Figure 43: Four Support Functions in an Integrated Outcomes and Assessment System

information and resources needed by individuals and committees to carry out their integrated functions of curricular design and approval, learning assessment, program review, and professional development. While all colleges store documents, the challenge is to store, organize, and maintain them so everyone has ready access to the most current versions.

Technology Support

When outcomes and assessment initiatives were first implemented in colleges, there were no software systems specifically built to support them. Each program created its own spreadsheets and databases to aggregate and store quantitative results; the use of graphs and charts was minimal.

How things have changed! There is now a plethora of digital software to support curricular systems, creating many new challenges that often exceed our capacity to make good choices. Here are two of the greatest challenges:

1. Seeing how systems can be integrated for multiple purposes

2. Ensuring that data, no matter where it is stored, is only used for its intended purpose

Because there are many technology options on the market to meet the needs of an outcomes and assessment system, selection and implementation are increasingly difficult tasks. Here are seven suggestions that should help.

1. Determine the purpose of the software, how it will support your processes, and who will use it. Involve users in the selection and implementation.

2. When defining the functionality of the software, include representatives from diverse programs and disciplines, especially those who have third party accreditation so a comprehensive list of functionality and data needs can be defined and documented in a

scoring guide. Figure 44: Scoring Guide: Assessment Software, on the following page, provides an example of criteria that can be used in assessing assessment software.

3. Screen potential products using the scoring guide to determine which vendors should be invited to demonstrate their product.

4. Define a process for comparing systems and make the selection.

5. Provide just-in-time coaching, training, and support for all users of the system.

6. Provide simple, clear "How-to" instructions that are focused on specific tasks (how to upload a learning artifact for learners; how to create surveys, scoring guides, rubrics, checklists for instructors; how to review the results of organization-wide assessment for instructors and administrators).

7. Assure that data can only be accessed and used for its intended purpose.

Scoring Guide: Assessment Software

Software System Reviewed:

Directions: Rate each indicator using the rating system below.

0—Absent   1—Weak   2—Adequate   3—Good   4—Exemplary

Factor: Usability	0	1	2	3	4	Notes
• Intuitive	☐	☐	☐	☐	☐	
• Simple/direct format	☐	☐	☐	☐	☐	
• Uses our same terminology/language	☐	☐	☐	☐	☐	
• Similar functions, etc. to current products	☐	☐	☐	☐	☐	
• Ease of navigation	☐	☐	☐	☐	☐	

Factor: Functionality	0	1	2	3	4	Notes
• Has embedded survey component	☐	☐	☐	☐	☐	
• E-portfolio component	☐	☐	☐	☐	☐	
• Can develop/administer tests	☐	☐	☐	☐	☐	
• Can share questions and aggregate data across surveys	☐	☐	☐	☐	☐	
• Can build assessment tools (checklists, scoring guides, rubrics, etc.)	☐	☐	☐	☐	☐	
• Can share tools across programs/courses	☐	☐	☐	☐	☐	
• Supports data comparison (previous to current)	☐	☐	☐	☐	☐	
• Provides search capability	☐	☐	☐	☐	☐	
• Can attach files (txt, pdf, etc.)	☐	☐	☐	☐	☐	

Figure 44: Scoring Guide: Assessment Software, 1 of 5

Scoring Guide: Assessment Software

Software System Reviewed:

Directions: Rate each indicator using the rating system below.

0—Absent   1—Weak   2—Adequate   3—Good   4—Exemplary

Indicators		0	1	2	3	4
	• Can attach media files (video, audio, etc.)	☐	☐	☐	☐	☐
	• Store and archive data	☐	☐	☐	☐	☐
	• Provides multi-user integrity (check in/out capability)	☐	☐	☐	☐	☐
	• Can make learners work public or private	☐	☐	☐	☐	☐
	• Can export data to other formats/products	☐	☐	☐	☐	☐
	• Can produce standard and custom reports	☐	☐	☐	☐	☐
	• Uses security/encryption	☐	☐	☐	☐	☐
	• Does not have a forced password change	☐	☐	☐	☐	☐

Factor: Integration with other products		0	1	2	3	4	Notes
	• Student Information System	☐	☐	☐	☐	☐	
	• Learning Management System	☐	☐	☐	☐	☐	
	• Placement System	☐	☐	☐	☐	☐	
Indicators	• Microsoft Office (Word, Excel, Powerpoint)	☐	☐	☐	☐	☐	
	• Microsoft Access	☐	☐	☐	☐	☐	
	• Curriculum Approval System	☐	☐	☐	☐	☐	
	• Instructional Design System	☐	☐	☐	☐	☐	
	• Clinical Tracking Program	☐	☐	☐	☐	☐	

Figure 44: Scoring Guide: Assessment Software, 2 of 5

Scoring Guide: Assessment Software

Software System Reviewed:

Directions: Rate each indicator using the rating system below.						
0—Absent 1—Weak 2—Adequate 3—Good 4—Exemplary						

Indicators		0	1	2	3	4	
	• Data Warehouse	☐	☐	☐	☐	☐	
	• Version compatibility with all systems	☐	☐	☐	☐	☐	
	• Limit for data storage	☐	☐	☐	☐	☐	
	• One login/share with other systems	☐	☐	☐	☐	☐	
Factor: Platform Supported		**0**	**1**	**2**	**3**	**4**	**Notes**
Indicators	MAC	☐	☐	☐	☐	☐	
	PC	☐	☐	☐	☐	☐	
	Web-based	☐	☐	☐	☐	☐	
	Externally hosted	☐	☐	☐	☐	☐	
Factor: Support		**0**	**1**	**2**	**3**	**4**	**Notes**
Indicators	Online help (screen)	☐	☐	☐	☐	☐	
	Online help (functional)	☐	☐	☐	☐	☐	
	Help reference documentation	☐	☐	☐	☐	☐	
	Training for users	☐	☐	☐	☐	☐	
	Training for trainers	☐	☐	☐	☐	☐	
	Phone support for product use	☐	☐	☐	☐	☐	
	Phone support for assessment coaching	☐	☐	☐	☐	☐	

Figure 44: Scoring Guide: Assessment Software, 3 of 5

Scoring Guide: Assessment Software

Software System Reviewed:

Directions: Rate each indicator using the rating system below.

0—Absent   1—Weak   2—Adequate   3—Good   4—Exemplary

Factor: Customer Service		0	1	2	3	4	Notes
Indicators	• Responsiveness during sales cycle	☐	☐	☐	☐	☐	
	• Customer reference checks	☐	☐	☐	☐	☐	
	• One key contact for support or call center	☐	☐	☐	☐	☐	
	• Process for systems down and reporting	☐	☐	☐	☐	☐	
	• Process for escalating issues	☐	☐	☐	☐	☐	

Factor: Stability of Vendor		0	1	2	3	4	Notes
Indicators	• Current install base	☐	☐	☐	☐	☐	
	• Customer list	☐	☐	☐	☐	☐	
	• User group available	☐	☐	☐	☐	☐	
	• Length of time in assessment field	☐	☐	☐	☐	☐	
	• Length of time product in the marketplace	☐	☐	☐	☐	☐	
	• Dates of product releases (major, minor)	☐	☐	☐	☐	☐	
	• Partnerships with other vendors	☐	☐	☐	☐	☐	

Figure 44: Scoring Guide: Assessment Software, 4 of 5

Scoring Guide: Assessment Software

Software System Reviewed:

Directions: Rate each indicator using the rating system below.

0—Absent   1—Weak   2—Adequate   3—Good   4—Exemplary

Factor: Cost Model	0	1	2	3	4	Notes
Indicators • One time fee + annual maintenance	☐	☐	☐	☐	☐	
• Per learner fee paid by institution	☐	☐	☐	☐	☐	
• Per learner fee paid by learner	☐	☐	☐	☐	☐	
• Training fees	☐	☐	☐	☐	☐	

Reviewer_____   Date_____

Figure 44: Scoring Guide: Assessment Software, 5 of 5

Allocation of Time

One of the greatest barriers to sustaining the outcomes and assessment initiative is the lack of instructor time to participate in the on-going cycle of planning for learning, assessing learning results, reviewing results, and making changes based on results. The work can't be done without the engagement of instructors. Remember, if nothing changes in the classroom, nothing really changes.

Here are three specific places to begin:

1. Recognize the correlation between support, time, and quality. We can't reduce one without increasing or decreasing the others. If increased quality is what we seek, an increase in time and support must follow.

2. Design professional development work sessions where staff not only learn about outcomes and assessment design, but actually *get work done on their courses.*

Here in PART SIX, we have explained the importance of the four core processes and their related support functions for creating and sustaining an integrated outcomes and assessment system, shown earlier on page 146 (Figure 43: Four Support Functions in an Integrated Outcomes and Assessment System.)

3. Allocate specific time and resources for instructors to be involved in curriculum planning and assessment.

Scenario: *We were recently in discussions with the academic leadership of a university that was well on its way in the establishment of an integrated outcomes and assessment system. We were there to work with them on finalizing their organization-wide learning outcomes and assessment tools.*

It became obvious early in the discussions that they lacked both people with time and technical support to sustain what they had begun to create.

During the discussion we talked about the correlation between time and support. We suggested that if the work needed to be completed in a short time frame, it would be essential to bring in other people and invest in more efficient software. If they couldn't invest in this kind of support, it would take much longer to get to an integrated system.

Although they desired additional outside help and better technology, they were constrained by budget and, in the end, decided to invest in training and release time for a few of their own people to move the work forward with the technology they had already invested in.

Integrating the People

We can talk about integrating process and support functions, but the one thing that is more important than anything else (and often more difficult) is getting people to work as one unit with the single purpose of creating the best possible learning experiences for learn-

ers. There are practical things we can do right away to build stronger connections among people who do the work. Here are the five that we have found most effective.

1. Sharing membership across committees and/or creating liaison roles.

2. Bringing the leaders and instructors together at the beginning of each academic year to share their plan for the year's work and discuss their common purpose.

3. Planning work sessions in which they do their work side-by-side in the same space.

4. Identifying professional development needs that are shared and participating in them together.

5. Creating small social events to celebrate together significant outcomes and assessment achievements of the college.

Assessing Assessment— Closing the Loop

I (Ruth) laughed when, as a young 27-year-old professor, I was appointed to my university's College Committee on Committees. I am not sure I was a very good member because I didn't understand the complexities of organizational systems. I wasn't yet able to see the layers and cycles that are inherent in every complex system—so I laughed.

It's the same thing when we begin to think about assessing an assessment system. It doesn't sound like a good place to go. But, in fact, it is a good place to go, and it is a natural conclusion to the work we have described throughout this Primer.

Assessing our Outcomes and Assessment System (don't laugh) simply means we look at our own work through the same critical lens through which we see the work of others—and other systems. We ask similar questions and gather data that reveals the outcome of the system we have constructed, and

use what we learn to change our system in significant and/or insignificant ways. When we have done this, we have completed one full cycle, and cycles continue.

Figure 45, Assessing the Effectiveness of the Core Curricular Processes and Figure 46, Assessing the Strength of the Support Functions for the Four Curricular Processes, on the following pages, are tools that can be helpful in assessing the four core curricular processes and support functions that make up an Outcomes and Assessment System. In addition to assessing the effectiveness of the core curricular processes and strength of the support functions, we suggest you also assess how well they are integrated. Keep in mind that design is needed when curriculum and assessment efforts are being integrated, and both need design support from all key players in the organization. Instructional designers are still the ones who can provide support and strength to such design efforts.

Core Curricular PROCESSES	WHO	HOW	WHEN
1. Curriculum Design & Approval	• Governance Committee • Advisory Committee • Instructors	• Survey • Observation • Quality of outcome statements • Review of time log	• Annually
2. Learning Assessment	• Assessment Committee • Instructors • Learners Program Outcomes • Advisory Committee • Program Managers	• Surveys and focus group w/learners • Assessing artifacts • Review the results of assessment • Facilitated discussions • Tracking, follow-up	• According to a schedule for each organization-wide outcome • According to a schedule for each program outcome • According to a schedule for pre-identified courses
3. Program Review	• Academic Leadership • Program Managers • Department Chair • Instructors	• Follow-up actions taken • Resources provided	• Every three years according to a schedule
4. Professional Development	• Everyone involved in all curricular processes	• Surveys • Review work session artifacts (COG, POG, Maps) • Focus group w/instructors • Review Learning Management System reports	• At the completion of work sessions • Annual review of number of instructors/staff involved

Figure 45: Assessing the Effectiveness of the Core Curricular Processes

SUPPORT	WHO	HOW	WHEN
1. Design Support	• Instructors • Instructional Designers	• Review the quality of the outputs of the design processes, curriculum, and assessment • Surveys and focus groups with instructors and instructional designers	• Annually, before the end of Spring semester
2. Documentation Support	• All users of documentation (Instructors, Instructional Designers, Deans, Dept. Chairs, Program Managers, etc.)	• Review user usage data produced by documentation system • Review currency of documents • Surveys and focus groups with all users of documentation	• Annually, before the end of Spring semester
3. Technology Support	• Instructors • Instructional Designers • Instructional Technologists	• Surveys and focus groups with instructors, instructional designers, and instructional technologists	• Annually, before the end of Spring semester
4. Allocation of Time	• Instructors • Instructional Designers • Instructional Technologist • Academic Leadership, Dept. Chairs, Program Managers, etc. (everyone involved in curriculum)	• Observations and reporting by key people involved in each process • Surveys and focus groups with all parties involved in each process	• Annually, before the end of Spring semester

Figure 46: Assessing the Strength of the Support Functions for the Four Curricular Processes.

PART SEVEN
Establishing and Sustaining Trust

*It's not about speed, it's about depth: sustainability
happens at the depth of trust.*

Cultivating Trust and Building Relationships

When I started my first full-time job in higher education, I expected the early days to be all about setting up a formal (outcomes and) assessment system, creating professional development for faculty and staff, establishing institution-wide assessment tools, etc. I was completely wrong! The first and most important piece of my job was cultivating TRUST and building relationships with faculty.

—Michele Yurecko, Ph.D.
Assistant Dean of Academic Assessment
The College of Saint Elizabeth

There is no more appropriate issue to address in these last pages of this Primer than the issue of trust. That's because leaders and administrators cannot implement an effective outcomes and assessment system without the trust of instructors. Because outcomes and assessment is about what happens in live and on-line classrooms between instructors and learners, instructors must trust that it is the *right thing to do* and trust those who *lead the change initiative over time.*

Through the six books in *The OUTCOME Primers Series 2.0,* we have sought to provide the knowledge base and processes necessary to develop an effective system of outcomes and assessment. In doing so, we are fully aware that in the minds of some instructors and administrators, outcomes and assessment can be a particularly threatening curricular change. So, everything we have written about in these six Primers hinges on taking the time to build relationships and trust.

I (Ruth) learned this lesson early, but perhaps, not early enough.

It was on the occasion of my very first consulting contract with a community college that was in the initial stages of developing program-level learning outcomes, that I made some bad assumptions. One was that my tenured position at the university gave me the credibility to walk into a community college and share my wisdom—the wisdom I had gained working with learners in graduate programs. I was completely wrong.

The second wrong assumption was that I thought everyone would love me, because I had been brought in by the powerful vice president of the college. (Do I hear a laugh?)

The first thing scheduled for my two-day, in-service contract was an early morning session with the deans and department chairs so I could tell them, first, what I was going to tell the instructors about outcomes and assessment. When I was about thirty minutes into the part about accreditation agencies asking for learning outcomes from every program, the humanities dean stood, slammed his fist on the table and shouted, "bull-%^#", and left the room.

Needless to say, I don't recall very much more about that meeting, but whatever I did must have worked, be-

cause at the end of the second day, an instructor approached me and said, "Congratulations! The instructors trust you. We don't normally take to university-folk. We consider them the control group for the wonderful new things we are doing in community colleges." Wow! That was an eye opener.

I returned to that college on many occasions to help them continue the work, but I was never fully aware of why they accepted me until I started reading about issues of trust. I wasn't perceived as one of them; in fact, like many university types, I had never actually even stepped foot into a community college until that day. As I look back now, I am amazed that they didn't have a whole lot of other words for me.

Why Trust is a Concern

Consultants and outside facilitators aren't the only ones who run into trust issues in colleges and workplace training programs. Trust issues occur within the ranks—and often because of rank. This is particularly true when it comes to learning outcomes and assessment where the success of the work depends directly on how much instructors believe in and trust the process.

In this work of curricular change, trust is a great concern. If instructors and staff don't trust the champions who lead the change, nothing changes where it really counts. We have to realize that instructors are the key persons in the system who actually guide learners and, in the end, *deliver the goods—the outcomes, the evidence.*

This realization is supported in Figure 47, The Three Levels of Outcomes, on the following page, which illustrates how the achievement of learning outcomes and the flow of learning evidence happens through courses in the system, the results of which end in improved learning for all, beyond that of the guidance of instructors. Even organization-wide and program level outcomes are achieved through the work

instructors do at the course level. It is the instructors who make it all happen. Without their trust, the kinds of changes we envision for the benefit of learners and the sustainability of this work will not happen.

Having expressed the importance of the instructor role, let's not neglect the important role administrators and other support staff play in creating trust in an integrated outcomes and assessment system.

The Three Levels of Outcomes

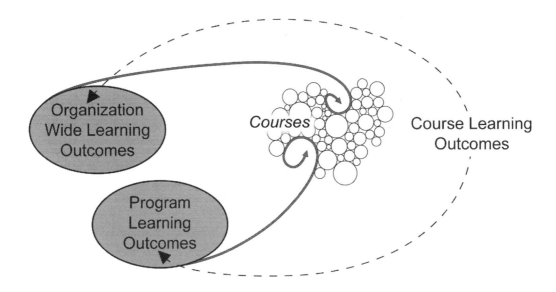

In the end, it is the course instructor who "delivers the goods."

Figure 47: The Three Levels of Outcomes

Establishing Trust

Regardless of who we are, or the position we hold in the organization, it is not wise to assume that the staff and instructors with whom we need to work automatically trust our *capabilities*, our *character*, or our willingness to openly *communicate* with them. According to experts on trust, there are three specific questions that most directly address degrees of trust in work relationships. We have applied them below to our work with outcomes and assessment.

1. How capable is this person in leading the outcomes and assessment work for this program/college?

More specifically,

- Is this person well-grounded in the concepts, skills, and issues necessary to develop a sustainable outcomes and assessment system in this program/college?

- Does this person have experience working with outcomes and assessment at the course, program, and organization level?

- Does the person have a clear vision of what we need to do to build on the outcomes and assessment processes we have already put in place?

These are particularly valid questions in higher education where we tend to put instructors from content areas into leadership positions that require *process* expertise. There is little rationale for appointing a Ph.D. in Economics to lead an outcomes and assessment initiative, unless that person has developed professional expertise in outcomes and assessment processes.

2. Does this person have the character needed to lead others?

What we really want to know with this question about character is:

- Do they do what they say they will do?
- Do they honor personal and professional boundaries?
- Do they keep agreements?
- Do they own their mistakes and make amends?
- Do they tell the truth?
- Do they act consistently?

3. **Is this person able and willing to communicate well with us and others?**

What we want to know from this question about communication is:

- Are they willing to share the skills they have?
- Will they withhold early judgment of us and our work?
- Will they openly build solid working relationships?
- Will they seek our input and the input of others?

It was Lewis Thomas (1973) who wrote: *We are all obsessed by the need to feed information in, as fast as we can, but we lack a sensing mechanism for getting anything much back.* Trust is built, in part, on an openness to receiving things back.

Sustaining Trust

The ability to sustain trust requires many of the same actions described above for establishing trust, along with a few more described below. It is possible to lose the trust that we initially establish over the smallest of things. The questions below are ones we should ask ourselves as we work to sustain trust over the long haul.

- Are we leading change in manageable increments?
- Are we sensitive to the workloads our colleagues carry?
- Do we spend as much time listening to the ideas of others as

we do to feeding others our own ideas?

- Do we trust others to have good ideas?

- Do we trust the ability of the team to realize our intended goals?

We'd like to leave you with a thought we found in our research on trust that might surprise you. It surprised us.

The primary benefit of trust, from the leader's point of view, is that it accelerates learning.
—Aubrey Daniels

Our Preferred Terms for Creating and Sustaining an Outcomes and Assessment System

Term	Meaning
Academic program	A highly organized set of learning experiences learners navigate through that usually culminates in a specific degree or certificate.
Accountability	The institutional responsibility to stakeholders for the results it produces. The institution defines its intended learning outcomes and provides appropriate information about results to key stakeholders.
Artifact	Something the learner produces that can be used to assess their learning. Also known as a work product.
Assessment	Ongoing process aimed at understanding and improving learning by systematically gathering, analyzing and interpreting evidence of intended learning outcomes.
Assessment cycle	The assessment schedule defined to assess each outcome. The cycle includes time for assessing, adjusting, and confirming/reassessing.
Assessment plan	Documents the types of assessment tasks and assessment tools that will be used to collect evidence of the learning outcomes. Also includes the cycle for each learning outcome. Assessment plans can be at the institutional, program, or multi-section level.
Assessment reports	Documents common themes, issues, conclusions and adjustments needed to improve learning. Assessment reports can be at the institutional, program, or multi-section level.
Assessment tasks	Complex and significant tasks learners complete to demonstrate the intended learning outcome (e.g. projects, portfolios, presentations, problem solutions, demonstrations, simulations, role-plays). Often referred to as performance tasks.
Competencies	A term mistakenly used as a synonym for outcomes. They consist largely of miniscule tasks the learner is asked to demonstrate.
Competency-based framework	A curriculum design approach that consists of demonstrating a set of specific isolated tasks for mastery of content to be learned.
Concepts	Ideas that learners must understand in order to achieve the intended learning outcome; emphasis on depth of understanding rather than breadth of information.
Content-based framework	A curriculum design approach which consists largely of topics to be covered, readings on the topics, term papers on the topics and objective tests about the topics.
Core systems	This system is at the very center of the organization's mission, the very reason it exists. Think processes of curriculum design, learning assessment, program review, and professional development that produce and improve curricular offerings which are what bring learners to the college.

Our Preferred Terms for Creating and Sustaining an Outcomes and Assessment System

Term	Meaning
Course Outcome Guide (COG)	A one-page plan focusing on intended learning outcomes and working backwards to determine essential course content.
Curriculum design and approval processes	A process for creating and approving course and programs, managing and tracking the curriculum as it moves through the approval process, as well as storing, retrieving, and reporting curricular information to other units. These processes are part of an Outcome and Assessment System.
Cycle	Exists whenever the output of a process becomes one of the inputs in the next cycle. Without a cycle there is no system, there is only an event.
Direct evidence	Learners show their mastery of learning outcomes through demonstration of skills, knowledge, and abilities.
Emergence	Continual adaption and change, which is a part of every living system.
Ground zero	The program-level is where all outcomes-based curriculum efforts should begin.
Indirect evidence	Perceptions or comparison data that allows for inferences to be made about mastery of learning outcomes, but does not demonstrate actual learning. Graduate and employer surveys are common indirect measures.
Integrated processes	Individual processes that are brought together to function as a coordinated whole around a specific purpose. Processes are sometimes referred to as sub-systems.
Interdependence	Dependence between two or more people, groups or things.
Instructor involvement	One of the four factors that sustains an Outcome and Assessment System. Instructors need to be involved in developing outcomes (course, program and organization-wide level), creating assessment tools, providing input to policies, co-creating processes, and helping other instructors.
Issues	Problems and challenges that learners must be able to resolve in order to achieve the intended learning outcome.
Leadership	One of the four factors that sustains an Outcome and Assessment System. Providing the direction, support and acknowledgement of outcome and assessment work. Leaders exist at the institution-level, program level and course (multi-section level). All levels are needed to implement an integrated Outcomes and Assessment System.

Our Preferred Terms for Creating and Sustaining an Outcomes and Assessment System

Term	Meaning
Learner centered	Methods of teaching that shift the focus of instruction from the instructor to the learner. It aims to develop learner autonomy and independence by putting responsibility for learning in the hands of the learners. Learning theory and practice is based on the constructivist learning theory that emphasizes the learner's role in constructing meaning from new information and prior experience.
Learner's journey	A flow of learning events that learners navigate through to achieve the intended learning outcomes.
Learning assessment processes	Involves collecting, storing, scoring, aggregating, analyzing and using evidence of learning to regularly improve programs and courses. Learning outcome and assessment processes are driven by learning outcomes at three different levels of the organization: organization-wide, program, and multi-section courses. These processes are part of an Outcome and Assessment System.
Learning outcomes	Statements that describe a vision of what learners will be able to do outside the classroom (in real-life roles) as the result of their learning. Learning outcomes are short, concise and detailed descriptions that provide the road map for guiding course, program, and organizational level learning.
Norming	Raters meet to discuss rubric levels, what does a 4 look like, a 3, a 2, and a 1? Rating an assignment to see if all raters assess the learning artifact at the same level. Also known as inter-rater reliability.
Outcome and learning assessment system	A network of curriculum design, assessment, professional development and program review processes that assure the continuous improvement of learning experience for learners.
Outcome-based education	An educational theory that bases each part of an educational system around outcomes. By the end of any educational experience, each learner should demonstrate the learning outcomes. Learning activities and assessments should help learners achieve the specified outcomes. The role of the instructor adapts into a facilitator or guide that supports and coaches learners toward the learning outcome(s).
Outcome-based framework	A curriculum design approach which begins with a vision of what we hope the learner will be able to DO outside and beyond the classroom, in real-life roles, with what s/he learns in a program, course or workshop/training.
Organization-wide learning outcomes	The learning outcomes that all learners should demonstrate by the completion of a degree. Also referred to as general education outcomes, success skills, etc., depending on the institution (college).

Our Preferred Terms for Creating and Sustaining an Outcomes and Assessment System

Term	Meaning
Professional development	One of the four factors that sustains an Outcome and Assessment System. Designing and implementing an outcome-based curriculum for all instructors and staff in the same manner that we design outcome-based learning experiences for our learners. Produces the energy and the institution's internal capacity to create and sustain an outcomes-based curriculum. It also is a key process that is part of an Outcome and Assessment System.
Program	A highly organized set of learning experiences that learners navigate and result in intended learning outcomes, with some leading to a certificate, licensure, or degree.
Program map	The organization and visual depiction of the learner's journey through learning experiences and assessments aligned to achieve intended learning outcomes; a systemic view of planned learning experiences—entrance to exit.
Program Outcome Guide (POG)	A one-page plan focusing on intended program learning outcomes and working backwards to determine essential content for a program.
Program review	Seeks to determine the continued relevance of a program and determine what is needed to maintain, expand or discontinue it. This process is part of an Outcome and Assessment System.
Qualitative data	Exhibit differences in quality rather than amount. Qualitative data are often generated during subjective assessment processes by subject-matter experts that make judgments and inferences about levels of learning and express the assessment in holistic narratives.
Quantitative data	Exhibit variance in amount rather than kind. Numeric scores are considered quantitative when the numbers show different levels of learning or achievement.
Reliability	The rate at which assessments are repeatable over time (by the same person—intra-rater reliability). Rating an assignment to see if all raters assess it at the save level (inter-rater reliability).
Role definitions	Clear responsibilities that are defined for each role in the Outcome and Assessment System.
Rubric	A rating grid that specifies the characteristics to be assessed and describes what each accomplishment level would include: a qualitative assessment instrument that synthesizes the standards to help evaluators classify learner work.
Scoring guide	A qualitative assessment tool that explicitly describes the standard of good performance to help the learner know what "good" looks like; can be used by learners, evaluators, or assessors to provide feedback to improve performance or a product.
Self-adjustment	Adjustment to oneself or one's environment.

Our Preferred Terms for Creating and Sustaining an Outcomes and Assessment System	
Term	**Meaning**
Skills	Abilities that are essential to the intended learning outcome(s), usually learned and mastered through practice and feedback. Combined with what the learner must understand (concepts and issues), these form the content of the learning experience.
Standards	Used to assess a process, a product, or both. Defines what "good" looks like. Documented in the form of a scoring guide or rubric. Also known as criteria, indicators, benchmarks and specifications.
Support functions	The four support functions that are essential in an integrated, mature outcomes and assessment system are design support (curriculum and assessment), documentation support, technology support, and the allocation of time.
Support systems	These systems provide support to ensure the organization is running efficiently. Think of things like technology, business and accounting, facilities, human resources, and housing. They exist to support the core college systems.
Sustainability tools	One of four specific tools with questions pertaining to the four critical factors that influence the sustainability of an Outcome and Assessment system. These questions are contextualized at the organization-wide, program, course (multi-section), and instructor levels. The tools provide a systems and an appreciative inquiry approach to examining the effectiveness and sustainability of each level.
System	A network of interdependent parts that serve a common purpose.
System integration	One of the four factors that sustains an Outcome and Assessment System. The efficient flow of ideas, energy and information among the different interdependent parts of a single system.
Trust	Belief in the competence, character and open communication skills of someone. It is a critical success factor in creating and sustaining an Outcome and Assessment System.
Validity	The degree to which the measurement aligns with the learning outcome. It measures what we want it to measure.
Work sessions	A group learning session where learners are immersed and working together toward a common outcome. Learning happens as part of the process so that it can be repeated in the future. Requires a competent facilitator that can plan a session and guide the learners toward specific outcomes.
Workshop Outcome Guide (WOG)	A one-page plan focusing on intended learning outcomes and working backwards to determine essential content for a workshop or training.

Fundamental Concepts

Introduction: There are six fundamental concepts in outcome-based education that are embedded in the Outcomes and Assessment system as described in this Primer. Here is a short description of those concepts.

1. Learner-Centered

The term *learner-centered* broadly encompasses methods of teaching that shift the focus of instruction from what an instructor does to what learners do. Learning takes on the form of a wide variety learning experiences and learner support strategies that are intended to address the distinct needs of learners. In the Primer Series we express this concept as shifting from *teaching* to *guiding* learners *and focusing on the learner's journey.*

2. Topics vs. Learning Outcomes

Prior to the late part of the last century, it was pretty much accepted that developing curriculum was a matter of dissecting the knowledge-base into *topics* to form courses. In reality, most of the time, textbook authors did it for us. In this topic-focused model, teaching came to mean lecturing on topics, reading on topics and testing learners on their knowledge of specific topics.

In an outcome-based model, curriculum design begins at a very different place. It does not begin with a list of topics, but rather, with a vision of what learners must be able to do in real-life roles with what they learn. Subject matter is derived from an analysis of that vision.

3. Outcomes-Based vs Competency-Based Curriculum Frameworks

The terms *competency* and *outcome* are often thought to have the same meaning in curriculum development, because, in contrast to covering topics, outcomes and competencies both describe what learners will be able to DO with what they learn. But in the larger context, they reflect very different theories about learning. Here is how:

Competency-based learning trended in mid-20th century based on the work of behavioral scientists who believed learning was a matter of stimulus/response manipulation. When applied to the curriculum it meant dissecting and reinforcing simple behaviors. Behaviorists believed that by breaking the curriculum into tiny, specific *competencies* learning would be increased. But today, most scientists understand that in taking something apart we lose the whole— the connections. What this means for curriculum development is that the curriculum is built around significant *outcome* statements, not lists of behaviors.

4. Designing Backwards—Outside-In

Outcome statements describe what learners should be able to do outside a classroom in real-life contexts. This means we begin at the end (the intended outcome) and from there make decisions about assessment strategies and content.

5. Assessing Learning: Assist, Advance, Adjust

There are three equally important purposes for assessing learning: 1) to assist the learner (feedback), 2) to make decisions about advancing the learner (grading) and 3) to adjust learning experience based on results.

6. Instructor as Guide

When we are clear about what learners need to achieve (outcomes), and clear that it is their journey (not ours), the word *guide*, rather than *teach*, best describes an instructor's role. While the term *teach* derives from a content framework, the term *guide* reflects a learner-centered, outcome-based framework.

One of the best ways we gain new insights into how Outcomes and Assessment Systems are sustained is by listening to the voices of those in the trenches. In this section we share with you the advice of four leaders working at different levels of the system.

Here are their responses to the following question:

What are the most important things you can do to sustain an outcomes and assessment system?

From a Provost

> **Develop a succession plan** which phases in changes in key positions such as president, vice-president of academic affairs, associate vice-president/dean of arts and sciences and coordinator or director of assessment.
>
> **Provide for an overlapping of the key administrators** so that the importance of continuity in the critical processes related to outcomes, curriculum and assessment can be clearly communicated.
>
> **Have a clear and firm long term plan** regarding organization-wide outcomes and assessment which states that key systems must be continued despite turnover of personnel.
>
> **Adopt a Board policy mandating continuity** in the implementation of the approved plan for outcome-based education and assessment.
>
> **Document** philosophy, policies, processes and procedures well for new persons in key positions.

Empower faculty through professional development, learning communities, councils and committees to lead.

Link critical committees that influence and impact learning outcomes by having one or more people serve on multiple or all committees.

Develop a shared vision and update it periodically.

Build a culture of inquiry and experimentation. Make it safe to experiment, learn and share.

Provide the opportunity for faculty to mentor each other.

Recognize and celebrate accomplishments.

Provide appropriate level of support to enable staff to meet the expectations.

Understand that this is a journey; believe and trust the process.

Recognize that defining and assessing student learning outcomes is some of the hardest and most important work of the college.

From a Director of Institutional Effectiveness about restarting a dormant assessment initiative

Model servant leadership. Each level of leadership must engage a servant leadership philosophy. Key components in this philosophy include: setting high expectations for your team and helping them be successful, empowering your team to lead and make decisions, praising successes and modeling how to learn from and adjust to setbacks, building honest and trusting relationships with your team, and it never hurts to bring chocolate to team meetings.

Develop a common language. We have found the power of metaphor, specifically the river metaphor, to be extremely helpful. Whatever method you choose to engage your constituents, everyone needs to be speaking the same language. Terms need to mean the same thing to everyone.

Honor the past but plan for the future. *This may be good advice for just about any initiative where there are still members of the old guard deeply invested in the success of the institution. We found it imperative and extremely helpful to acknowledge the work of the past and build upon the foundation that had been laid. Enlisting the help and learning the history from those who laid the foundation taught us how to avoid some pitfalls that had been previously experienced and enabled us to gain much needed buy-in across the institution.*

Surround yourself with people who want to move forward. *Diversity within a team is critical to ensure that you have the complete perspective of the institution. With that in mind, it is also imperative at the beginning to surround yourself with people who want to move forward. If a team consists of too many people who want to wallow in the mud, no progress will be made.*

Meet people where they are and build from there. *We found that even with repeated and consistent messaging we cannot assume that everyone understands. Often it takes that personal touch, often with multiple personalized messages, to help concepts sink in.*

Use tools that are friendly. *Complicated or convoluted tools/forms will only serve to turn people off and hurt any momentum you've built.*

Communicate frequently and in a variety of formats. *We have used news-letters, presentations, one-on-one meetings, branding of the movement to create instant recognition and a web-presence to communicate our work.*

Maintain momentum. *Keep people engaged year round. Do not allow for the lull of a season to stop progress.*

From a Director of Learning Outcomes and Assessment

About Leadership

> **Identify an executive sponsor** that will champion student learning outcomes and provide needed support and recognition.

> **Identify a collaborative leader** that will be dedicated full time to lead, manage and support the day-to-day operations and activities related to student learning outcomes. Identify a backup person for continuity.

> **Establish a Steering Committee** composed of faculty and administrators that is charged with improving learning outcomes development and assessment.

About Committees

> **Establish common language** about outcomes and assessment.

> **Establish realistic/practical yearly action plans** that can be accomplished.

> **Research and benchmark** with other institutions.

> **Adopt methodologies that have worked** and adapt/modify them to fit your own culture and systems.

> **Link new systems to existing systems**. Integrate and align them.

> **Pilot new systems** and technology before adopting.

> **Provide just-in-time coaching** and support when implementing technology.

> **Nurture programs through modeling.**

> **Involve advisory committees.**

> **Use 3rd party facilitators** when appropriate.

From the Chair of a Curriculum Committee

Communicate the "why." *If staff do not understand why this process is important and what purpose it serves, they don't invest in it.*

Be a facilitative leader. *This work takes a leader who is not intimidated by the intelligence of diverse members and are comfortable harnessing their intelligence for the greater good. Be willing to listen to and rely on skills and expertise of the group.*

Create a safe environment. *For staff to speak up, ask questions, and share their thoughts, they need to feel like they are valued and respected.*

Set clear expectations from the start. *Clarify responsibilities and allow staff to excuse themselves if they are unable to meet the expectations. Assure staff that everyone has a shared responsibility for the process and ideas to improve it.*

Own the process. *If you are the Committee Chair over a core curricular process you should be involved in co-creation and improvement of the process as well as communicating what supports are needed.*

Value time commitment. *This means starting and ending meetings on time as well as providing the first five minutes to reconnect with each other and share news. It also means taking the time to get everyone's input before important decisions are made.*

Provide training and support. *Training should be focused, purposeful and hands on. Provide a big picture of the process, then provide guidance the first time through the process and finally ask for feedback on how to make it better.*

Provide an active role for everyone. *Making sure everyone has a clear role is vital to the process. Staff become committed to each other and take pride in their involvement.*

Co-create changes that are needed. *Use the expertise of group members to create drafts and prototypes. Involve members in the refinement.*

Let everyone know their work is valued—be grateful. *Even though they "signed up" for the committee and you expect them to meet their responsibilities, hearing appreciation and gratitude for contributing their time, expertise and being part of something important provides value for everyone, especially the students.*

Continually ask for input to improve the process. *Ask committee members for their improvement ideas and reach out to stakeholders to get feedback on their experience with the process. Take time at the end of the year to determine needed improvements and how they will be implemented.*

Mentor your successor. *Even if the member who succeeds you has been on the committee before, it's much different being in a leadership role. Meet with the successor and provide the big picture of the process from the leadership view point. Be available to answer questions as they arise. Provide support without taking away responsibility.*

NOTE: This facilitator guide is excerpted from *The OUTCOME Primer: Envisioning Learning Outcomes*.

Purpose

Before beginning to create learning outcomes, it is important to be clear about the full purpose of this activity.

The purpose is to stimulate conversation that results in a few significant learning outcomes that can drive what we do in face-to-face and virtual *classrooms*. These statements will clearly describe what we intend for learners to be able to do beyond and outside the *classroom* as a result of the work they do inside the *classroom*. It is the single most important step in building an outcome-based learning experience. While the tool can be used in any organization for adult education, as well as at any level of the organization, our example here focuses on a certificate or degree program but could just as easily be a course or workshop. We chose to talk about program first, because course or workshop outcomes are usually derived from clear and robust program learning outcomes.

Prepare prior to the work session

1. Identify the program you are going to work with.

Sometimes the word *program* is misunderstood. Think of it as any unit of learning that exists for the purpose of helping the participants achieve specified learning outcomes. A program usually consists of a series of learning experiences (courses, workshops, seminars, internships, tutoring sessions) through which a learner progresses. Because this is a very broad definition of program, in colleges it extends to include learner success and student support offerings provided by student services. In an outcome-based college curriculum, there is no distinction between academic services and student services. It is our sole business to help students realize important learning outcomes. In the workplace it extends from new worker orientation to top management training. In our terms, it is a *program.*

2. ***Identify the life role(s)*** in which you see the participants using what they learn in this program.

In technical and professional programs (industry or academic) this is relatively easy. Often, the title of the program defines an intended employment role(s) in a clearly identified industry group. It is also easy for college programs like developmental education, English as a Second Language and lower division transfer programs, where the role is often seen as one of *lifelong learner* or successful student in the next level of their educational experience.

Liberal arts programs in colleges are often much broader in the scope of life roles focusing on the roles of parent, family member, citizen in a democratic society, community member, global community member, steward of the environment, or all of them.

3. ***Expand your planning team.***

In addition to the trainers or instructors in this program, be sure to invite persons who have a first-hand view of the role(s) for which the participants/students are preparing. (You may already have an advisory group that fits this purpose.) You don't need large numbers. **What you do need are persons who have diverse insights into the expectations the learners will face *out there* in the defined role.** Choose individuals who are knowledgeable, articulate and interested in the success of the learners in the context with which they are familiar. Keep the number manageable. **A group of 6–12 participants is ideal.** With more than 15, it becomes difficult but not impossible.

4. ***Invite the participants.***

You want diverse perspectives. In a college setting, resist only inviting instructors. In an agency, reach out to persons who receive services from the agency. In business, include clients. In addition to giving participants the time, place and length of the work session (1.5–2 hours), be sure to tell them why they are important to this process. Their contribution will be greater if they know why they are there.

5. ***Gather the materials you will need.*** (Put your computer away. You need paper, pencil and good eye contact.)

- Flip chart or whiteboard for yourself.
- One sheet of note paper for each participant: 8½ x 11.
- Flip charts or whiteboards for the group. Up to 8 persons can work at one white-board, or two sheets of flip chart paper attached to a wall surface. The surface size should be at least two charts wide—overlapping slightly to form one continuous surface. If you have over 8 participants, divide your group and prepare two or more boards.
- Post-it® Notes. The 3 x 3-inch notes are sufficient. Choose any single color in quantities of 20 per participant.
- Masking tape (unless you have self-adhesive flip chart sheets).
- Pen or pencil for each participant.
- Markers, pens (Sharpies®) and/or crayons for participants.

Facilitate the work session

(Time: 1.5–2 hours)

1. ***Get set—before others arrive.***

- Arrange the room so the chairs are around the group's flip chart or whiteboard. Leave space for participants to stand around the board.
- Write the following at the top of each flip chart or whiteboard:

    –The role(s) this program is preparing the students or trainees for, if the role is obvious. If not, wait.
    –This question: **What do learners (in this program) need to be able to DO *out there* that we're responsible for *in here* (in this program, workshop series,**

course series)? (You might want to print this question on a large banner and post it on the wall for the whole session.)

2. Start the work session.

- Introduce yourself and talk briefly about the purpose of the work session. Put it in context of the mission of the organization.
- Acknowledge the different participants and what each brings to this work.
- Illustrate what is meant by learning outcomes by repeating the exercise you were asked to do in Part Two of this Primer: Pass out paper and crayons or markers. Have each participant begin in a corner of the sheet of paper and start slowly to draw overlapping circles, as you saw in Figure 5, (page 24) progressively getting larger and faster, letting the point of their crayons/markers *spin off* with the centrifugal force. Now have them draw it again and think about what it feels like— the engagement they feel—the momentum that is generated—the increased speed as they get to the outside edges of the paper. Note that this is what is meant by learning outcomes—with each new learning experience, we cycle from ignorance to insight, ignorance to insight, until we reach a level of mastery and spin out to apply what we have learned to the rest of life.
- Have participants create a *zoomer* by taking a Post-it® Note, folding it in half twice, and tearing a hole in the folded corner. Ask them to open up the *zoomer* and hold it close to one eye (with their view *zoomed out*) to see the entire landscape through the hole. This position is essential for envisioning learning outcomes. Now ask them to extend their arms further and further out until they can extend them no further. They will see only a small detail of the landscape through the hole with the context around that detail obscured by the paper. Explain that this position is often the limited view of what has been seen as traditional teaching with emphasis on *knowing* and not *doing*. We begin creating learning outcomes by moving the *zoomer* close to our eye (with our view

zoomed out)—envisioning what learners need to be able to DO in the rest of life that we are responsible for in the classroom, program, degree, or training.

3. Raise the two big questions:

What role(s) will this program impact? Discuss until you have consensus.

What do learners (in this program) need to be able to DO *out there* that we're responsible for *in here*?

Seed some answers. Write a sample answer to the question on a Post-it® Note and put it on the chart under the question just like you will ask them to do. Ask them to give another sample answer or two, until you are certain the instructions are clear.

Note: Emphasize early that each statement must describe an action, not a topic.

4. Start the BRAINSTORMING

- Ask everyone to stand and move to the chart. (*Some will want to sit, but do what you can to get them on their feet for this part of the work. The energy level will be higher when they stand.*)
- Ask them to close their eyes and actually envision what the person is doing in that role (1–2 minutes). As an option, ask them to use their zoomer, moving it out to see in more detail answers to the above two questions under 3 above: Raise the two big questions.
- Give them three rules for this activity, as they write their thoughts onto their respective Post-it® Notes:

  ○ RULE 1: Begin every statement with an action word; no single-word answers.
  ○ RULE 2: Read each answer out *loud* as you slap it on the chart.
  ○ RULE 3: Don't discuss answers.

- Tell them to GO—fast!!!!!!! (15–25 minutes).
- Tell them to STOP—when they have nothing left to contribute.

5. Monitor the BRAINSTORMING Carefully

Look for the following:

- Topics instead of action words. Help them make the change.
- Low participation. Seed possible ideas.
- Disengaged participants. Read some of their answers out loud to stimulate more thought.
- Stop only when there are no more answers.

6. CLUSTER the responses

- Ask the team to discuss and cluster the items on the Post-it® Notes into 4−10 groupings according to what they have in common.
- This is a collaborative process that will take another 15−20 minutes.

Suggestions:

- If there is disagreement about where something belongs, have them make a duplicate and put it in more than one place.
- If some don't fit, have the participants put them to the side or eliminate them with the consent of the person who wrote it.
- Encourage new answers that may arise.
- Encourage them to try more than one way to cluster.
- Let the group decide when they think they are done. Then, check to see that they have at least 4 and no more than 10 clusters. This is not a hard and fast rule, but it will make the rest of the work easier. If there seems to be good reason for more or less, go ahead with their number.

Ask them to circle each cluster with their red felt marker when they have consensus. The following graphic is what your "work in progress" should begin to look like.

7. *Work with the entire group to draft an 'action' OUTCOME STATEMENT for each cluster.*

Note: This is the most difficult part of the process—and the most important. To facilitate this part of the work, you must be familiar with the characteristics of good outcome statements discussed earlier in this Primer and shown in Figure 10 (page 41).

- Work with the group to draft an outcome statement (beginning with an action word) that synthesizes the essence of each cluster—one at a time.
  - Work with them to find the right action word—try many suggestions.
  - Keep the language clean and direct.
  - Keep asking: "Does this statement express what we can expect them to be able to do? Is it clear what we mean? Does it reflect what is in this cluster?"
- Stop when you feel you have enough input from the whole group at this time. Don't expect the group to go beyond a first draft of the outcome statements.
- Rewrite the draft statements on your flip chart for all to see.

The Work in Progress

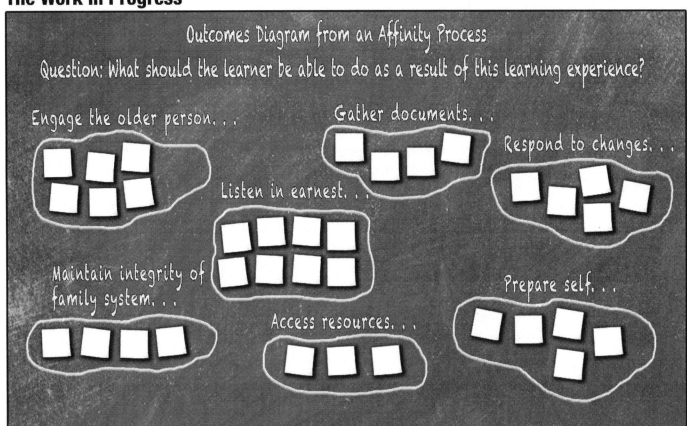

Outcomes Diagram from an Affinity Process

Question: What should the learner be able to do as a result of this learning experience?

Engage the older person. . .

Gather documents. . .

Respond to changes. . .

Listen in earnest. . .

Maintain integrity of family system. . .

Access resources. . .

Prepare self. . .

Conclude the work session

1. ***Agree on a timeline*** for continuing to work on the outcome statements. Not everyone will want to continue to be involved. Thank them for the contribution they have made.

2. ***Agree to take the lead on refining the statements*** unless there are others who volunteer. If a group wants to do it, keep the group small.

3. ***Refer to the examples and suggestions in Part Three under section titled,*** "Improving Your Outcome Statements," (starting on page 40) and Figures 10, 11, and 12 in improving these draft statements. The challenge is to capture the essence of each cluster.

4. ***Don't throw anything away.*** You will need all the Post-it® Notes as clustered by the group. If they are on flip charts, you can roll and carry them away. If they posted the notes on a whiteboard, you will need to move them to flip chart paper in their clusters to take with you. It is a good idea to take a photograph of the work as a record before dismantling it.

Create the FIRST DRAFT after the work session

There are three parts to this work which you can do as the facilitator, or which a team of 2–3 persons can do together.

1 Refine the OUTCOME STATEMENTS. You should have 4–10 statements drafted that reflect the clusters the group developed. Put these on several pages like Figure 11 that include program title, role descriptions, major concepts, followed by the outcome statements.

2. Organize the Post-it® Notes. Organize and list all of the statements made

on the Post-it® Notes that appear to fall under each cluster. There will be some notes that don't seem to fit anywhere. It's fine to eliminate them. The task here is to try to create a document that reflects the intention of the group, but you will need to bring greater order to it. Expect to reword many of the items. (Figure 11 shows the outcome statements that were derived from the ideas generated during a brainstorm process.)

3. Identify 2–4 major concepts (words or phrases) that seem to summarize what all the outcomes are about. (See Major Program Concepts in Figure 11 (page 42).)

Distribute the FIRST DRAFT to all those who participated

Follow through on a revision process, working toward 4–8 final outcome statements.

We recommend that you refer back to Figure 13 and use the scoring guide to assess the quality of your outcome statements. In Appendix A of this primer you will find sample outcome statements from academic and workplace educational programs generated through this process.

Debriefing Your Work Session

Even though we have provided fairly complete instructions for this tool, you will learn to facilitate it well only with experience. We have used this tool with hundreds of curriculum groups and are always surprised by the different things that happen.

To help you think about what happened in your session, we have summarized some of our own hard learned lessons. You might want to compare notes.

This list of related readings will give you a sense of the breadth of writings that have emerged over the last two decades that have influenced this work. While some reflect the trends in educational literature, many more reflect the trends in science and organizational development. All of these works have helped us think more systemically about teaching and learning in the context of a "greening" society.

Ecological Thinking—Natural Systems

Benyus, Janine M. (1997). *Biomimicry*. New York: Harper Collins.

Capra, Fritjof. (2002). *The hidden connections: Integrating the biological, cognitive, and social dimensions of life into a science of sustainability*. New York: Doubleday.

Capra, Fritjof. (1996). *The web of life: A new scientific understanding of living systems*. New York: Doubleday.

Frances, Robert. (2003). *Deep Immersion: The experience of water*. Vermont: Green Frigate Books.

Johnson, Steven. (2001). *Emergence: The connected lives of ants, brains, cities and software*. New York: Scribner.

Lawton, Rebecca. (2002). *Reading water: Lessons from the river*. Virginia: Capital Books.

Wheatley, Margaret & Kellner-Rogers, Myron. (1996). *A simpler way*. San Francisco: Berrett-Koehler.

White, Richard. (1995). *The Organic Machine*. New York: Hill and Wang.

Visual Design, Thinking and Tools

Banyal, Istvan. (1995). *Zoom*. New York: Viking.

Damelio, Robert. (1996). *The Basics of Process Mapping*. New York: Productivity Press.

Lakoff, George & Johnson, Mark. (1980). *Metaphors we live by*. Chicago: University of Chicago Press.

Nisbett, Richard. (2003). *The geography of thought: How Asians and Westerners think differently and why*. New York: Simon & Schuster.

Volk, Tyler. (1995). *Metapatterns: Across space, time and mind*. New York: Columbia University Press.

Systems Thinking—Organizations

Cohen, Arthur M. (1998). *The Shaping of American Higher Education*. San Francisco: Jossey-Bass Publishers.

Gall, John. (1975). *Systemantics: How Systems Work and Especially How They Fail*. New York: Quadrangle/The New York Times Book Co.

Meadows, Donella H. (2008). *Thinking in Systems*. Vermont: Chelsea Green.

Locke, John L. (1998). *Why we don't talk to each other anymore: The de-voicing of society*. New York: Simon & Schuster.

Lucas, Peter; Ballay, Joe; & McManus, Mickey. (2012). *Trillions: Thriving in the Emerging Information Ecology*. New Jersey: John Wiley & Sons. Inc.

Pink, Daniel. (2006). *A whole new mind: Why right-brainers will rule the future*. New York: Penguin Group.

Sanders, Irene T. (1998). *Strategic thinking and the new science*. New York: Simon & Schuster.

Senge, Peter M. (1990). *The fifth discipline: The art and practice of the learning organization*. New York: Doubleday.

High Performing Organizations

Esque, Timm J. (2001). Making an Impact: *Building a Top-Performing Organization From the Bottom Up*. Georgia: CEP Press.

Binder, Carl. (1998) *The Six Boxes: A Descendent of Gilbert's Behavior Engineering Model*. Performance Improvement. *http://www.sixboxes.com/_customelements/uploadedResources /SixBoxes.pdf*

Clark, Richard E. & Estes, Fred. (2008). *Turning Research into Results*. North Carolina: Information Age Publishing Inc.

Gerson, Richard F. (2006). *Achieving High Performance: A Research-based Practical Approach*. Maryland: HRD Press Inc.

Gilbert, Thomas F. (1996). *Human Competence: Engineering Worthy Performance*. Maryland: International Society for Performance Improvement.

Stiehl, Ruth & Bessey, Barbara. (1994). *The green thumb myth: Managing learning in high performance organizations* (2nd ed.). Corvallis, Oregon: The Learning Organization.

Wheatley, Margaret J. (2002). *Turning to one another: Simple conversations to restore hope to the future*. New York: Simon & Schuster.

Change and Sustainability

Adams, Marilee. (2015). *Change Your Questions Change Your Life*. California: Berrett-Koehler Publishers.

Gribbin, John. (2004). *Deep simplicity: Bringing order to chaos and complexity*. New York: Random House.

McCarthy, Michael. (2011). *Sustain Your Gains*. Georgia: Performance Management Publications.

Loehr, J. (2007). *The Power of Story: Change Your Story, Change Your Destiny in Business and in Life*. New York: Free Press (Simon & Schuster, Inc.).

Marlowe, Bruce A. & Page, Marilyn L. (2005). *Creating and Sustaining the Constructivist Classroom,* (2nd ed.). California: Corwin Press, A Sage Publications Company.

Mezirow, J.D. (2000). *Learning as Transformation: Critical Perspectives on a Theory in Progress*. San Francisco: Jossey-Bass.

Patterson, Kerry; Grenny, Joseph; Maxfield, David; McMillan, Ron & Switzler, Al (2008). *Influencer: The Power to Change Anything*. New York: McGraw Hill.

Senge, Peter; Scharmer, Otto C.; Jaworski, Joseph & Flowers, Betty Sue. (2004). *Presence: An exploration of profound change in people, organizations and society.* New York: Doubleday.

Quinn, Robert E. (2004). *Building the Bridge as You Walk on It.* California: John Wiley & Sons.

Zemsky, Robert. (2013). *Checklist for Change: Making American Higher Education a Sustainable Enterprise.* New Jersey: Rutgers University Press.

Leadership

Covey, Stephen M. R. (2008). *The Speed of Trust: The One Thing That Changes Everything.* New York: Free Press (Simon & Schuster, Inc.)

Daniels, Aubrey C. & Daniels, James E. (2007). *Measure of a Leader.* New York: McGraw-Hill.

Quinn, Robert E. (1996). *Deep Change.* San Francisco: Jossey-Bass.

Curriculum Development and Outcome-Based Design

Allen, Michael W. & Sites, Richard. (2012). *Leaving ADDIE for SAM: An agile model for developing the best learning experiences.* Alexandria, Virginia: American Society of Training and Development (ASTD) Press.

Bloom, B. S.; Engelhart, N. D.; Furst, E. J. et al. (1956). *Taxonomy of educational objectives: The classification of educational goals. Handbook 1: cognitive domain.* New York: David McKay Company.

Caine, Renate N. & Caine, Geoffrey. (1994). *Making connections: Teaching and the human brain.* New York: Addison-Wesley.

Costa, Arthur L. & Liebmann, Rosemarie. (1997). *Envisioning process as content: toward a renaissance curriculum.* California: Corwin Press.

Kirkpatrick, D.L. & Kirkpatrick, J.D. (2006*). Evaluating Training Programs: The Four Levels.* California: Berrett-Koehler Publishers.

Kirkpatrick, D.L., & Kirkpatrick, J.D. (2007). *Implementing the Four Levels: A Practical Guide for Effective Evaluation of Training Programs.* California: Berrett-Koehler Publishers.

Prickel, Don & Stiehl, Ruth. (2017). *The GUIDING Primer: Guiding Toward Learning Outcomes.* South Carolina: CreateSpace.

Stiehl, Ruth & Decker, Michele. (2017). *The CONTENT Primer: Aligning Essential Content with Learning Outcomes.* South Carolina: CreateSpace.

Stiehl, Ruth & Null, Lynn. (2017). *The ASSESSMENT Primer: Assessing and Tracking Evidence of Learning Outcomes.* South Carolina: CreateSpace.

Stiehl, Ruth & Sours, Lori. (2017). *The OUTCOME Primer: Envisioning Learning Outcomes.* South Carolina: CreateSpace.

Stiehl, Ruth & Telban, Kathy. (2017). *The MAPPING Primer: Mapping the Way to Learning Outcomes.* South Carolina: CreateSpace.

Discipline Integration

Barrow, John D. (1995). *The artful universe: the cosmic source of human creativity.* Boston: Little Brown and Co.

Wilson, E.E. (1999). *Consilience: The unity of knowledge.* New York: Alfred A. Knopf.

Acknowledgments

Our thanks go to the hundreds of individuals in colleges, agencies and industry who, through our teaching and consulting experiences with them, have helped to shape our understanding of learning outcomes and assessment over the years. Without these experiences, we would have had nothing at all to say.

As just one part of a six-part series, this Primer wasn't created by us alone. We are deeply indebted to our full team on *The OUTCOME Primers Series 2.0. :* Don Prickel, Lori Sours, Lynn Null, Michele Decker, Geoffrey Floyd, Katy Krupp, and Robin McBride. This team has never failed to inspire us. They have each demonstrated a high level of intellectual honesty concerning our work and have paddled the rapids with us on the way to the *take-out.*

Additional credit goes to the educators and administrators at Cuyahoga Community College for engaging with us in this work and being committed to outcome-based education. We had many opportunities to work together and implement the concepts and ideas expressed in this work. We are glad you invited us into your raft. Special acknowledgement goes to Dr. Marilee Adams whose work on question thinking and an inquiry mindset influenced our inquiry approach in these Primers.

Sustainability is a never-ending journey. We invite all those that are committed to this endeavor to work together to continue to share and learn from each other.

—Kathy Telban
Ruth Stiehl
2017

Kathy Telban, CPT, SPHR, M.Ed.

PRESIDENT, CHIEF OUTCOME STRATEGIST AND COACH, iSOLVit LLC

PAST BOARD MEMBER, WHITE WATER INSTITUTE FOR LEADERSHIP TRAINING

FORMER DIRECTOR OF CURRICULUM DEVELOPMENT AND LEARNING OUTCOME ASSESSMENT, CUYAHOGA COMMUNITY COLLEGE

Kathy Telban is a multi-dimensional professional with over 20 years of industry experience in information technology, technical training, sales, human resource, workforce development and organizational effectiveness. She has spent the last decade in higher education designing, implementing and improving outcome-based education and assessment processes. In addition to holding in-house administrative positions, she has coached college faculty and administrators in systems planning across the US and Canada. Kathy is particularly passionate about helping organizations improve their outcomes where everyone matters, which is the key tenet of her company, iSOLVit. Kathy lives in Cleveland, Ohio and can be reached through *www.isolvit.org* and/or *www.outcomeprimers.com*.

Ruth E. Stiehl, Ed.D.

PROFESSOR EMERITUS, INSTRUCTIONAL SYSTEMS, OREGON STATE UNIVERSITY

CO-FOUNDER, WHITE WATER INSTITUTE FOR LEADERSHIP TRAINING
FOUNDER, THE LEARNING ORGANIZATION

Dr. Stiehl, a thought leader on learning outcomes assessment for over twenty years, was lead author on the acclaimed original series of *THE OUTCOME PRIMERS*. Over a period of fifteen years this original series guided colleges across the United States and Canada as they prepared for new accreditation standards for outcomes assessment. Along with a team of new co-authors and consultants at The Learning Organization, she has expanded the work beyond colleges to workplace training, including agencies, business and industry. In contrast to the work of many academics, all of the writing, speaking and workshops produced by The Learning Organization are charged with story, metaphor, and integrated learning. Dr. Stiehl lives and works in Corvallis, Oregon.

Authors can be contacted at *strategists@outcomeprimers.com*.

Don Prickel, Ph.D.
EXECUTIVE EDITOR

Dr. Prickel, one of the lead authors in the Outcome Primers Series 2.0, has also served in the major role of executive editor for all six primers, assuring continuity within the series. He brings to this work many years of experience as an adult educator and consultant to colleges and universities on instructional strategies and adult learning theory.

The authors of *The OUTCOME Primers Series 2.0* are available to consult in person with you and your organization in the following ways:

- Facilitating work sessions in outcomes and assessment planning at any level of the organization
- Face-to-face and on-line coaching, advising, and providing counsel to leaders, committees, and instructors on outcomes and assessment

Contact us through our website:
www.outcomeprimers.com
or
email us at: *strategists@outcomeprimers.com*

Made in the USA
San Bernardino, CA
26 August 2018